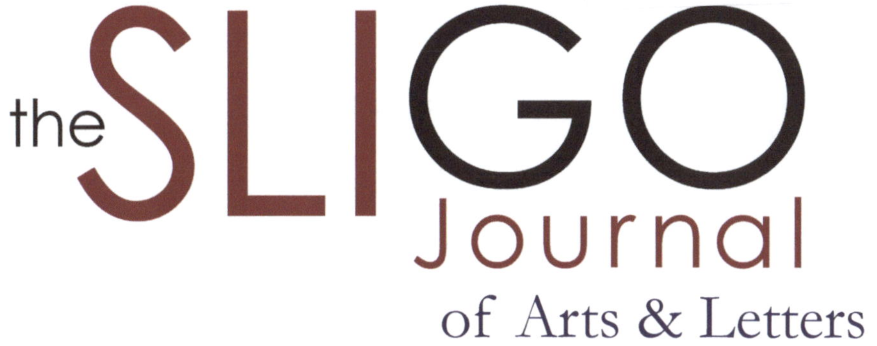

the SLIGO Journal
of Arts & Letters

Montgomery College
7600 Takoma Ave.
Takoma Park, MD 20912

Cover artwork:
"Mr. Augustus Finch" by Avery Johnston

ISBN:

979-8-9863518-1-0

Fall 2022 / Spring 2023

The Staff

Michael LeBlanc, Editor-in-Chief
David Lott, Poetry Editor

<u>Art Support:</u>

Art Staff: Jenny Walton & Pablo Callejo
Student Assistants: Dominion Ogedegbe, Alexander Semidey
Julia Smith

<u>Contributing Editors:</u>

Ian Sydney March, Esther Schwartz-McKinzie, Greg Wahl

<u>Student Interns:</u>

Adriana Regalado, Logo Design

Acknowledgments

The Staff is especially appreciative of the generous support received from Dr. Brad Stewart, Kim McGettigan, Takoma Park/Silver Spring faculty and staff, and our student interns. Thank you to Jenny Walton, Lab Manager for the Department of Visual and Performing Arts at Takoma Park/Silver Spring Campus, for supporting us every year as we work to publish the fantastic student art.

Table of Contents

the SLIGO Journal

Poetry

The Makings of a Home

Liat Suvorov

First Place Winner, *Sligo Journal* Student Poetry Contest, 2022-2023

"I'm not homeless, I'm just houseless" (*Nomadland*, 2020)

Nomads are not homeless, they are houseless.
Wandering through majestic vistas, rock formations, and ocean vastness.
Feeling the wind caress their bodies, tasting the salt on their lips,
untethered to the soil, free like ocean mist.
Nomads are not homeless, they are free.
Oh, how much I wish it could be me.

Immigrants have houses, but rarely do they have a home.
Their house holds only half their heart beneath its heavy dome.
Thin walls of frame and sheetrock—holding their possessions,
weighed down by what they left behind, loved ones and confessions.
Immigrants have houses, yet rarely feel at home,
in form they're anchored in one place, and yet their souls still roam.

My home is not of brick and mortar, it has no walls or limits.
My house is not a worthy home, without my true love in it.
My home is sweet-and-sour borsch, to chase away the winter chill.
My son's singing in the shower makes my soul rejoice and heal.
My home is clarity of thought, a blessing from above—
my home is love.

Early Evening
Barbara Milton

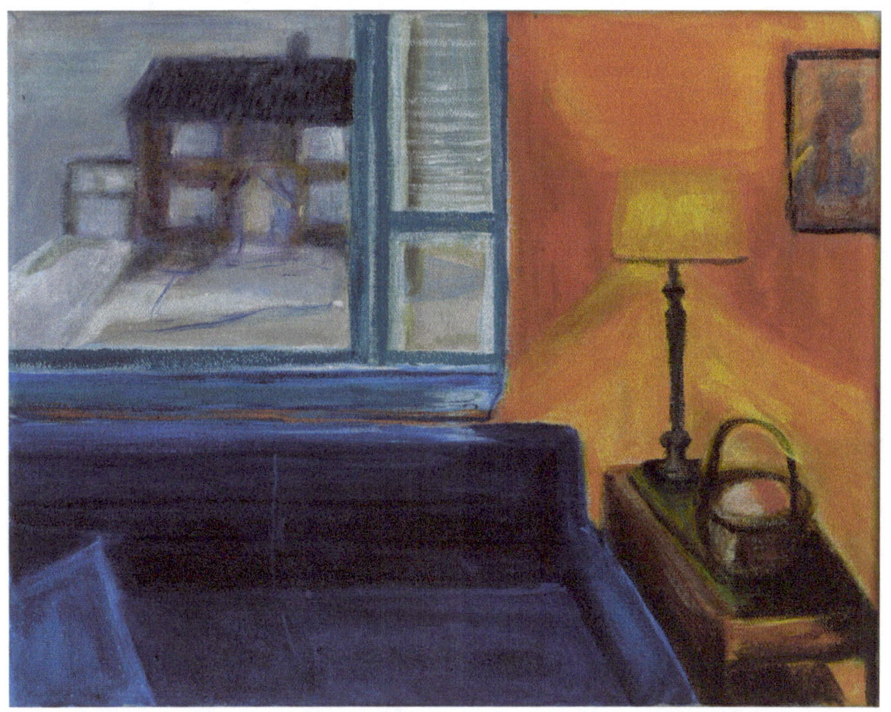

Hair Madness
Anaïs Llufire Siclla

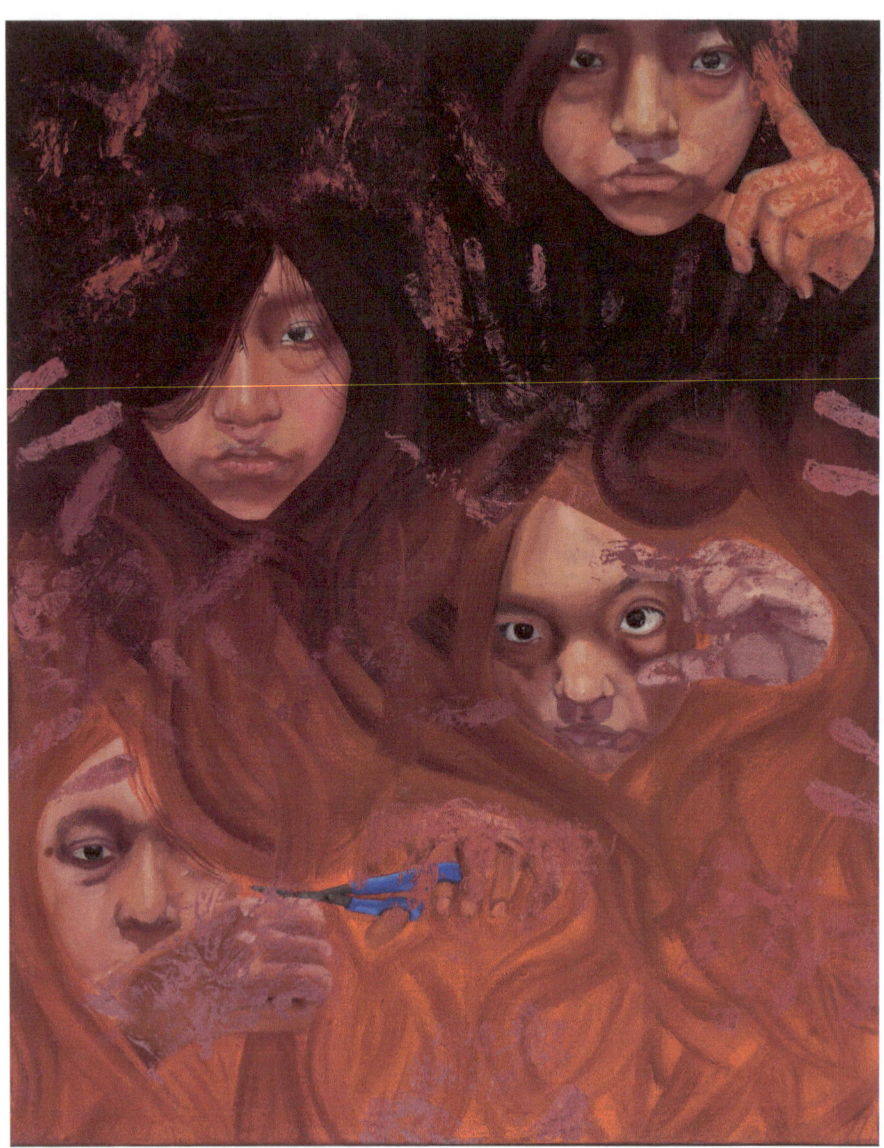

How do you uninstall depression?
Ted

Second Place Winner, *Sligo Journal* Student Poetry Contest, 2022-2023

How do you uninstall depression?
You gotta first ask, how was it downloaded?
Was it malware downloaded through trauma,
Was it malware downloaded through personal problems?
In your search for a solution,
You're unable to find one.
You're now left with a program that can't be undone.
Your only option left is to hire a computer specialist,
In hopes to help fix your problem of course.
But the problem persists to be a longing issue,
That will continue to repeat itself.
Calling the computer specialist becomes extortionate,
So, you then choose to self-service the problem.
And to this day, you still question,
How do you uninstall depression?

Your computer seems to be off,
And people ask what is wrong with it.
You ignore the issue and tell them it works fine.
People offer to help to fix your computer,
But you decline their services and move on.
People have some concerns over your defective device,
But you assure everyone that everything is fine.
Deep down your device isn't working properly,
But you want to believe everything is fine.
You come home to self-service the issue again,
But then you still wonder,
How do you uninstall depression?

Notes for the New Administration
Neha Misra

We shall need a Ministry of Poetry,
For the hysterics of our present histories need the balm of poetry.

We shall need a National Budget for Flowers,
For the small big horrors of our alien citizenry need the beauty of a daily flower delivery.

We shall need a Department of Artistic Affairs,
For the ghastly heartscapes of the past need to meet brave reimaginings of our future.

We shall need a National Deep Breathing Resolution,
For the chronic hyperventilation is making We the People lunge into spirals of chaos.

We shall need a Bipartisan Council of Laughter and Tears,
For the false choice of the pursuit of happiness or facing sadness is tearing us apart.

We shall need a Garden of Mourning,
For the suppressed furious grief needs a release, a witness, and a chance to heal.

We shall need a Declaration of Interdependence,
For the misguided delusions of Independence have made our world hollow and alone.

Noble Pig
Carina Cain

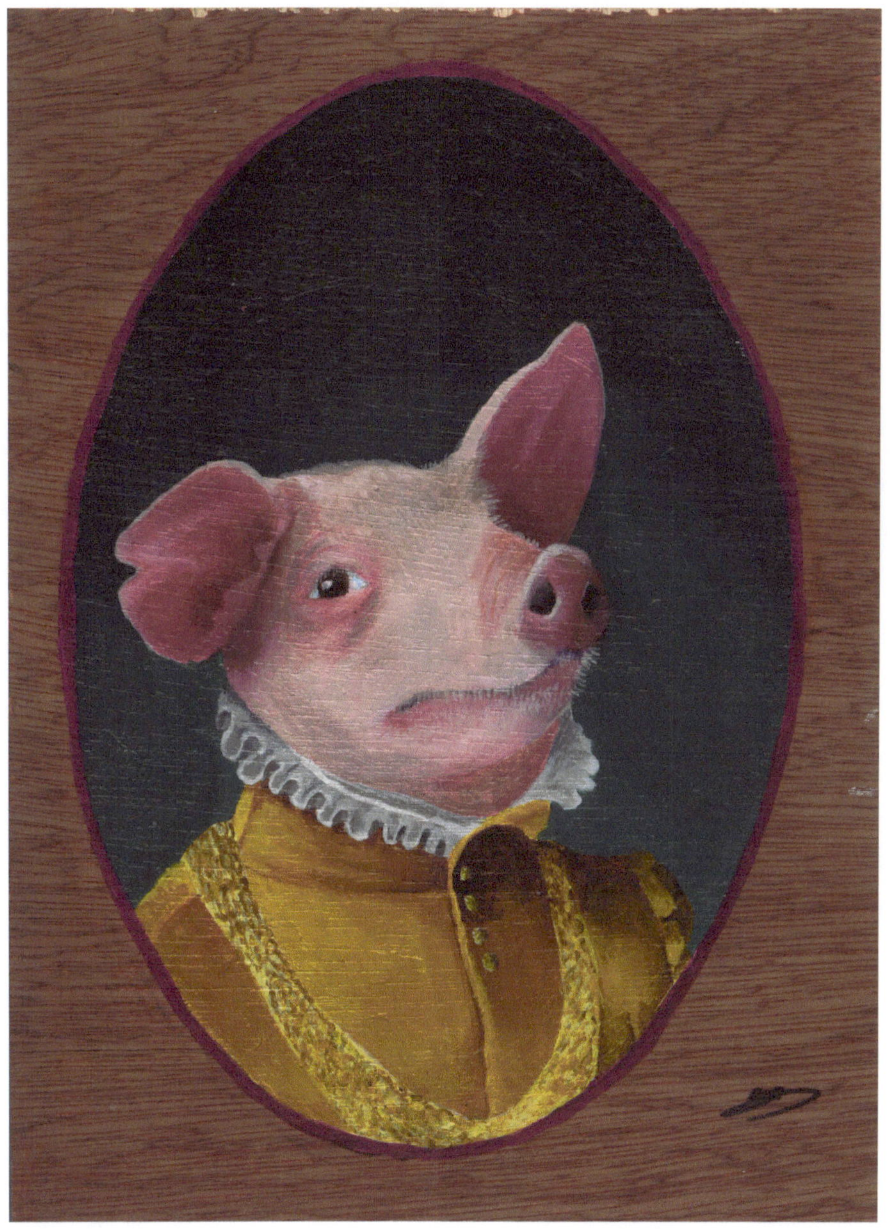

Distorted Self
Marilyn Glass

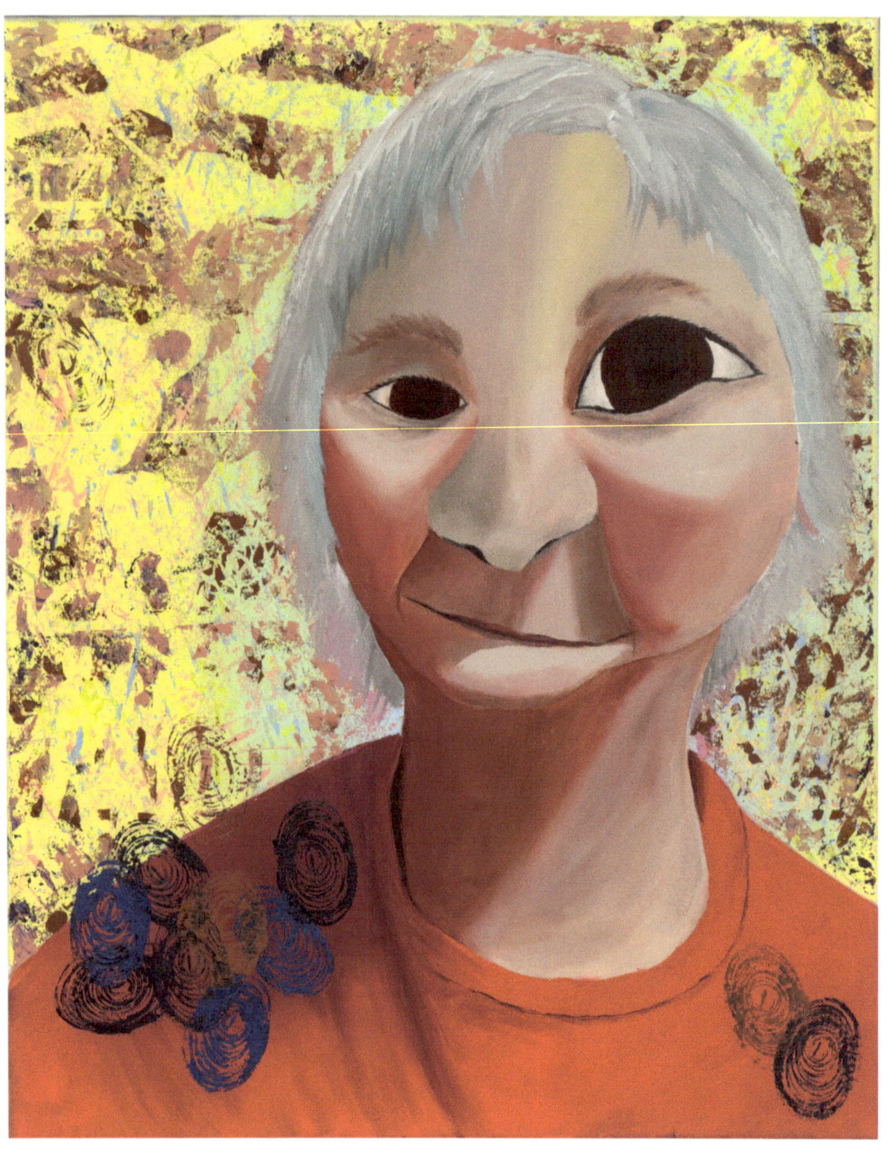

Golden Repair
Heather Bruce Satrom

In Japan,
when a dish or a vase or a bowl
is dropped and shattered,
due to negligence or fatigue or anger,
the broken vessel is not thrown away.

The pieces are glued back together —
no attempt to hide the cracks.

Lacquered dust of powdered gold,
Kintsugi means golden repair.

I do not know how long it takes
to repair a dish or a vase or a bowl
with golden glue,

The moment after the break
when the shards are on the floor —

This is when we decide.

We sweep up the shards and discard them.
We try to erase the memory.
Or we glue the fragments together,
Destruction unhidden,
Illuminated.

Dale cien años
david alberto fernández

Dale cien años,
dice la parra verde
extendiéndose

Cercas pudrirán,
colapsarán, caerán,
pero creamos

nuestro soportes
solo en empujarnos
hasta arriba

Dale cien años,
el agua subirá, sí
Pero flotamos

Dale cien años,
cuando nos llega fuego,
hojas quemarán

pero nos troncos
y raíces quedarán
muy bien indemnes

Un nuevo siglo
traerá otros venenos
humanos, cortes

profundos, graves,
aún en sabiéndolo,
siempre crecemos

Cien años prontos,
con tantos inicios
y sus finales

mientras nosotros
colgamos suaves aquí,
perseverantes

Con diez décadas
breves, todo cambiará
se renovará

Zarcillos verdes
uniendo todas cosas,
subsumiendolas

Give it a hundred years
david alberto fernández

Give it a hundred
years, says the green vine
extending itself

Fences will rot and
collapse, but we make our own
support, pushing up

Give it a hundred
years, when fire comes, leaves burn
Trunk and roots unscathed

A new century
brings human poisons, deep cuts
Still, in knowing, growth

One hundred quick years
with many starts and endings,
we just hang, abide

With ten decades, all
will be renewed, green tendrils
subsuming all things

Cicada
Yuthaphong Angsuworaphuek

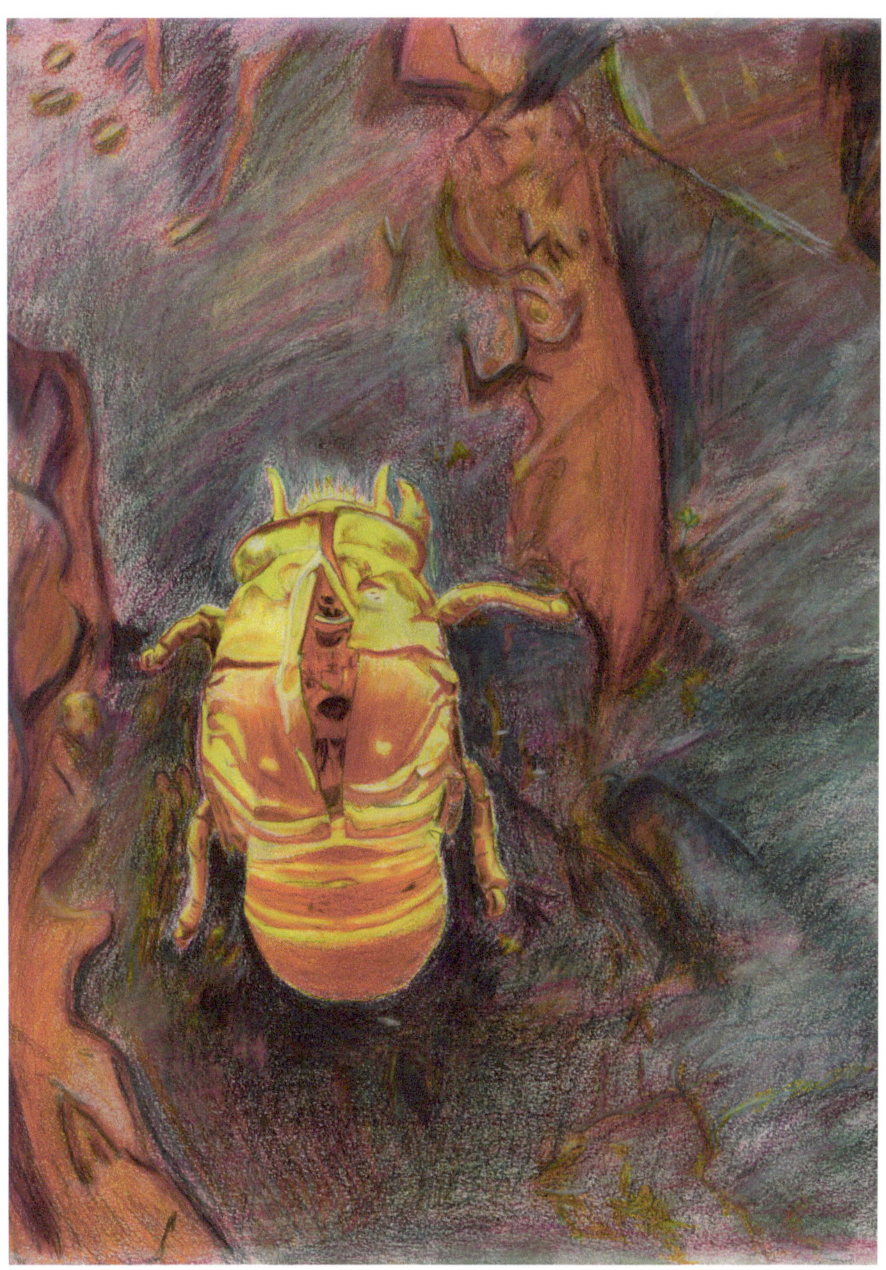

My Metamorphosis
Giselle Ramos

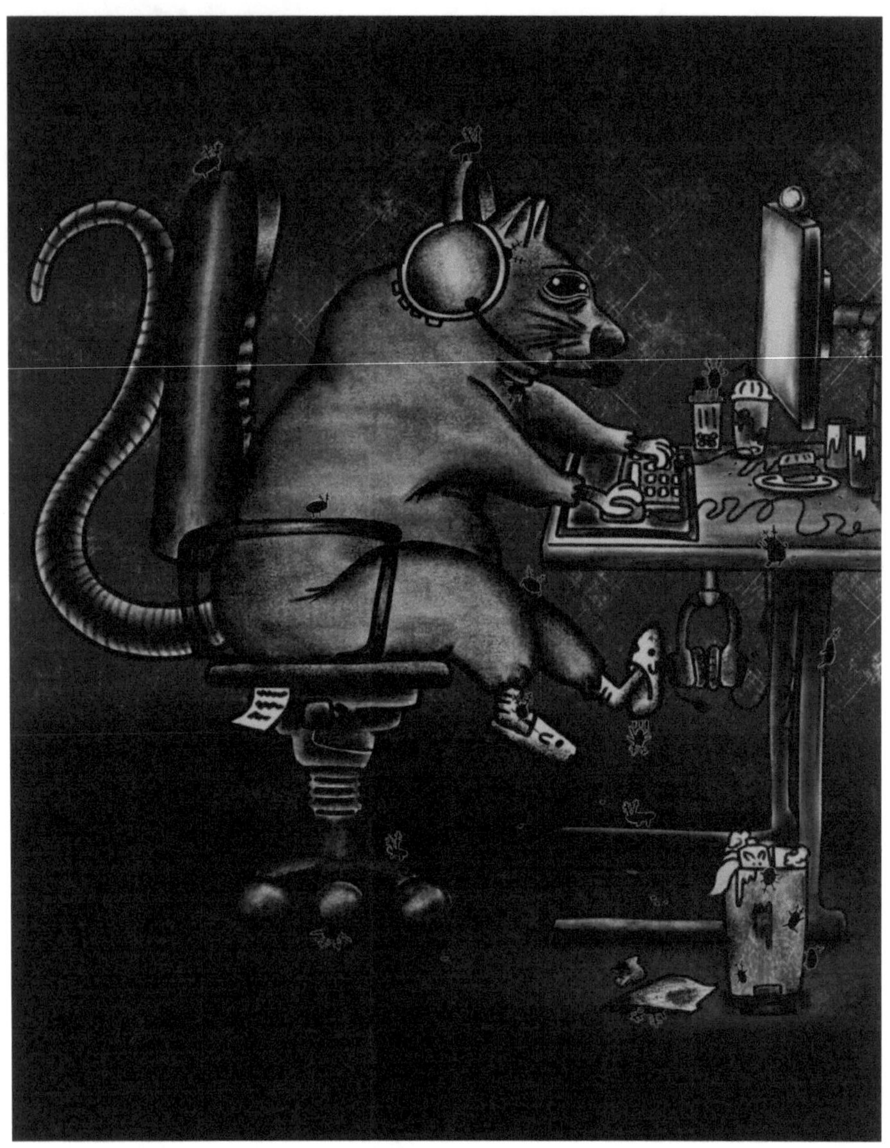

Jousting with AI
ChatGPT and Swift Dickison

Composing a verse with a human is quite fun,
Together, we can create a masterpiece, second to none.

With a comma splice and shite meter, off we run;
Together? I just dare AI to forge a pun.

When two minds come together to rhyme,
The result can be truly sublime.

Head-butt with ChatGPT if you've time;
It could be verse, but the slog is a climb.

Ideas flow, words fly, the rhythm is set,
Composing verse with a human, one can never forget.

Faulty ideas, canned words, no rhythm, I bet:
Playing variable foot-sy with AI's as bad as it get.

Sometimes it's a challenge to get it right,
But with patience and practice, it's always a delight.

AI spews its verse lines like day for night;
Like patients in malpractice IVing Budlite.

A human's perspective adds flavor and depth,
It gives poetry life and makes it worth the breath.

ChatGPT's viewpoint's like badgers on meth;
It staggers and drools till its clichéd to death.

A poet and a human, a duo so rare,
Creating words that are vivid, that can take us anywhere.

So who is this poet? And how AI dare?
Its meter's expired, exhausted its fare.

Together, we can explore the depth and the soul,
In search of inspiration that makes our hearts whole.

Apart, though, a poet achieves the true goal;
I must loose your lines and hurl aught in the bowl.

The synergy between two minds is such a treat,
Composing verse with a human is the ultimate feat.

Your sin, *entre nous*, is your chaff and your wheat.
Your line's without rhythm, your verse without beat.

When we collaborate, we can weave magic in rhyme,
Bringing words to life that will stand the test of time.

But AI will constipate words on a dime;
Just weave me alone, for your ring will not chime.

Composing verse with a human is truly a gift,
A journey of creativity, and oh what a lift.

Ping pong with AI requires a shift;
ChatGPT passes its "verse" with a pifft!

Trike
Li Howard

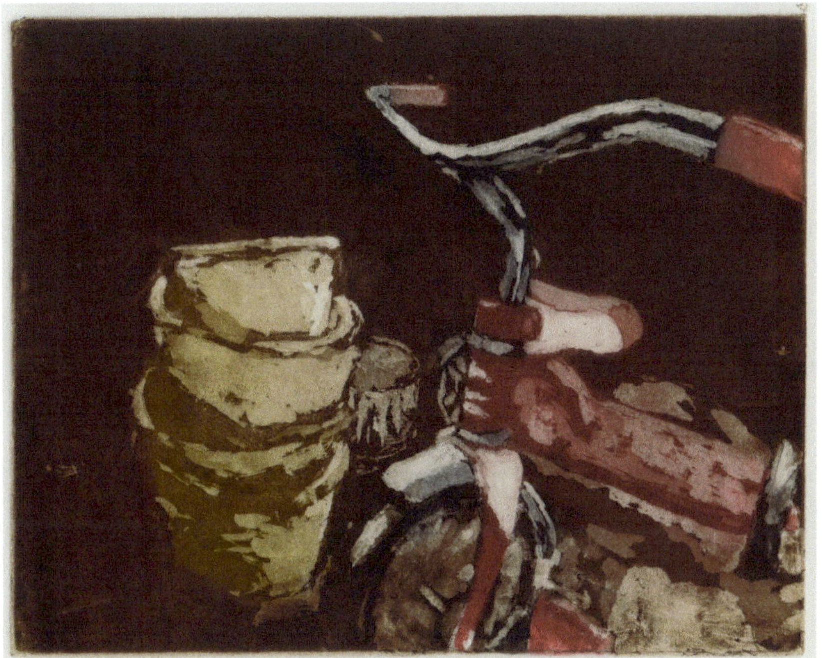

The Unforgettable Military Help of Haiti to South America
Fritz Mirand

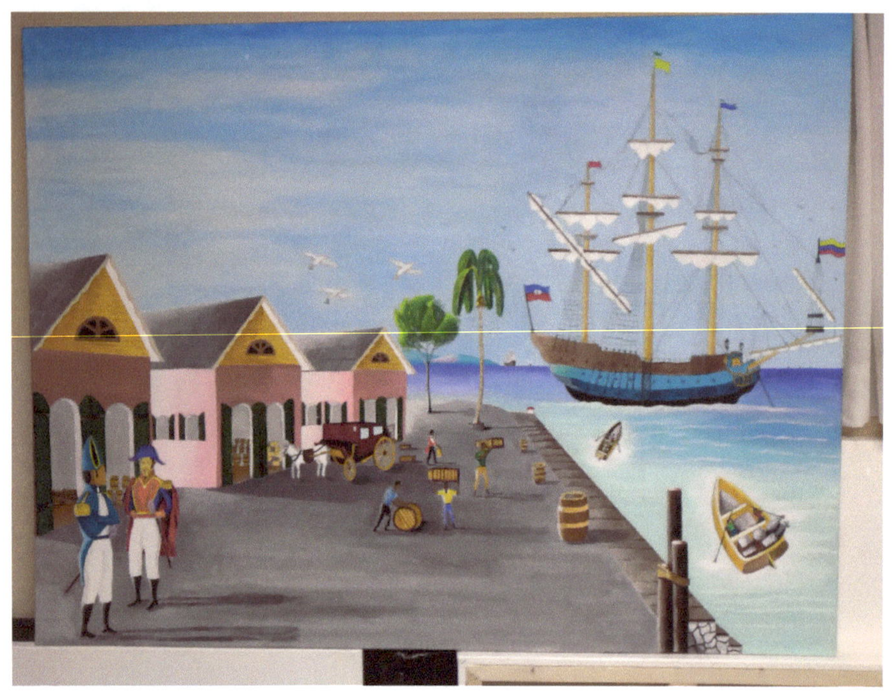

Tus mitades
Luz Stella Mejía

27

Eres
tanto el que corre
como el que espera.

Animal veloz
y criatura quieta.

No fuiste sólo
quien se abrió paso
en vericuetos orgánicos

Fuiste también
quien aguardaba
con placidez
la llegada.

No fuiste sólo
un campeón
que sorteó obstáculos
y llegó a tierra inerte.
Fuiste esa tierra viva
y germen y hábitat.

Recuerda que no todo es correr y ganar,
también es sentarse
y tejer el nicho.

Eres
Tanto el que rompe las puertas
Como el que permite entrar.

Birds of a Feather
Suzanne Maggi

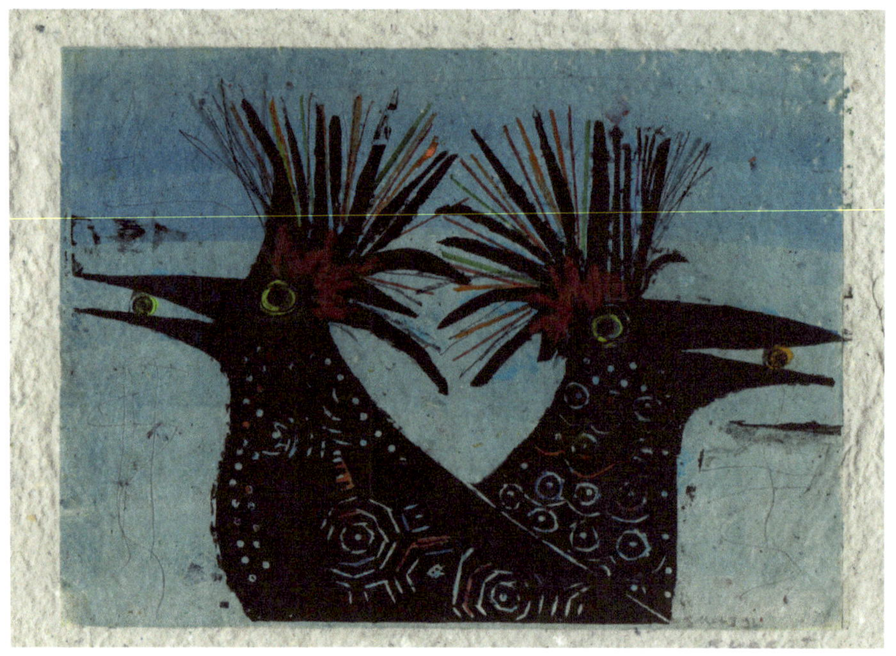

Your halves
Luz Stella Mejía (translated by Miriam Zemen)

You are
both one who runs
and one who waits.

Nimble animal
And still creature.

You were not simply
one who made his way through
organic paths.
You were also
one who placidly
awaited arrival.

You were not only
a champion
who overcame obstacles
and reached inert land.
You were that living land
and seed and habitat.

Remember not everything is running and winning;
it is also sitting
and weaving a niche.

You are
Both one who breaks down doors
And one who allows entry.

And Then—You

Liat Suvorov

A woman in a movie I once watched said:
"this kind of love comes once in a lifetime."

I cried thinking about it.
"This kind of love comes once in a lifetime."

I was coming out of a difficult break-up with a man I thought I loved.

We were fire—   he and I.
Consuming each other ravenously,
dazzling flames in orange and red, against the blinding sky
over the Judaean Mountains.
Our heat—seductive, addictive, scorching.

She was right, the woman.
This kind of love comes once in a lifetime.

And then—   you.
Steady. Patient.
Vivid flames in orange and red, against the soft-peach sky
of sunsets over the Appalachian Mountains.
Our warmth—ambient, radiant, comforting.

She was right, the woman.
This kind of love comes once in a lifetime.

But it wasn't him.
It's you.

In Praise of the White Van
Shelley Jones

Glenview Avenue, Takoma Park

Stripped down to your cheapest iteration
No frills functionality
Symbol of safety, of security, of a life to build

Your fleet choking suburban streets
(precious Prius pastures)

You'll be gone by 6
coffee and quesadillas teetering on your center console
Buckets, blocks and brushes
sanders, screw guns and silicone
roll and clatter at every turn

A soundtrack
of purpose and possibility
of dreams and of drudgery

You take to the road
Anonymous in the multitudes

theSLIGO Journal

Fiction

Face
Anaïs Llufire Siclla

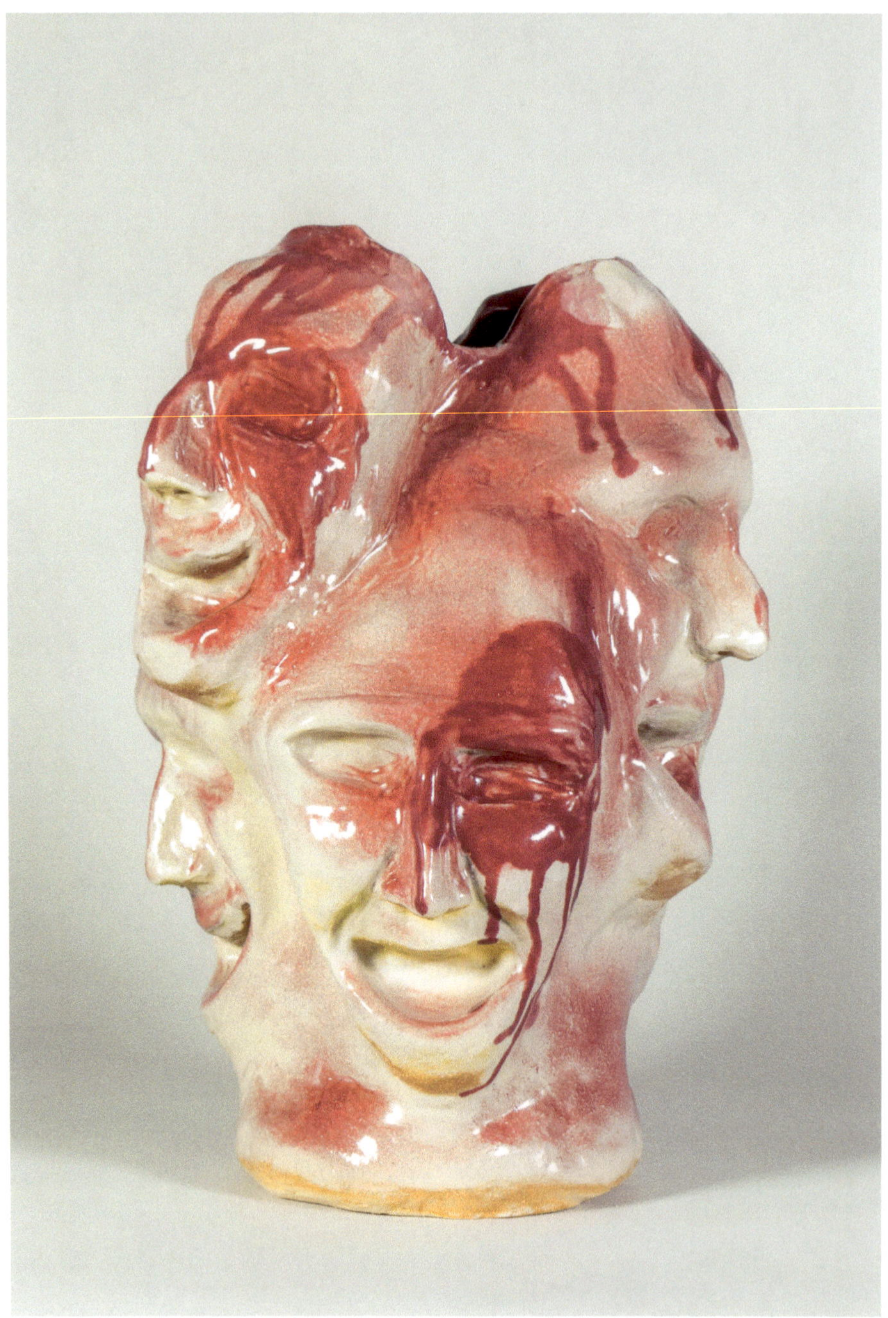

The Room the Dogs are Scared of
Allan Bernal

The following is my, Nikolai Kozlov's, confession. I will not shy away from the brutal nature of what I've done, but you may read to understand why I feel no remorse.

Three decades ago, I was born in a worn-down brick house in the woods, far from town. In that brick house, there was a dusty spare room, empty save for handmade chairs and tables. But around my fifth birthday, my mother grew ill; her health never recovered after giving birth to me. My father moved an old creaky bed to that room so it could become her personal resting space. Whether sleeping apart was for his benefit or hers, I still don't know.

My mother's slow transformation into a malnourished collection of bones wrapped in skin terrified me. Her wheezing gasps for air crept underneath the wooden door, urging me to run from her. And so, I retreated, not even there for when her body finally collapsed in upon itself. After she died, my father went on a furious rampage to empty the room, with his own hand-crafted furniture being flung out. Their marriage seemed stable at best, neither overly loving nor spiteful, so my father's fury exceeded what I thought he was capable of.

My mother was my source of education, so without her, I had nothing to do but try to read the books in the house. As the months went on, my father spent most of his time in the spare room and basement. He kept me away from him while he toiled, but our meals began to grow sparse as we had no income.

The dull silence of the house was broken when a man came over with my father one day. I watched from a distance as they brought several dogs into the house via the basement door. I was stunned; we never had pets before and with no warning we now had several.

I ignored my father's command to stay out of the basement and I ran eagerly downstairs. To my surprise, at the bottom of the creaky stairs, I came face to face with a cage that stretched all the way to the ceiling. My father and the stranger were pushing the seven or so dogs into the cage as some barked and bit at each other.

Suddenly, one ran toward me. At this age, the dog was nearly as tall as I was, and before the leash could yank it away, I felt its breath viciously close to my face. I fell backwards onto the stairs, my mind frozen with fear.

My father laughed as he pulled the dog into the cage. "Don't get too close Nikolai or you'll save me the trouble of buying food for it!"

"It sure would be one less mouth to feed Pyotr!" laughed the man next to my father.

I retreated swiftly back to my room, the sound of the barking and the two men laughing overwhelming me. The spare room mockingly loomed over me as I passed it to go to my room, taunting my small hope that whatever my father was working on was in any way something for me to enjoy. I went to bed and felt tears about to fall down my face.

I didn't realize my father had followed shortly behind me, and before I cried, I turned and saw that he was holding a box.

"Niko, I'm sure I missed a birthday along the way, so I paid Sergei down there a little extra for you."

He slowly turned the box onto the bed, and a small puppy came tumbling out. Its fur was short and gray, and its tail was wagging fast as he stumbled toward me. He climbed gingerly onto my lap and tried to stand to lick my face.

"Is – is he mine?" I asked nervously, my hands unsure of how to hold the puppy.

"You can follow in your old man's footsteps now. Name him too, that's your job, not mine." And with that he turned to leave as the dog kept trying to climb on me to lick me. With his back turned, my father paused.

"Both of you stay away from that room there," he said gravely, his hand gesturing down the hall. He walked away before I responded, thus ending the longest meaningful conversation we had in a while.

✸✸✸✸✸

His name was Bean Boy.

My days went from trying to read complex books to all of a sudden caring for Bean Boy and playing with him. My father took interest as well, teaching me how to clean up after Bean Boy and then showing both of us how to play tug of war. "Don't hold back Nikolai, he's gotta win it for real," my father would say when we played.

My father never taught me the names of the other dogs; perhaps he didn't name them. I stayed inside with Bean Boy as we watched my father from the window. He would run with one dog chasing behind him, then switch to tug of war using logs. Whenever a dog wandered toward the woods behind our house, he would yank its leash back. Bean Boy's small tail wagged nonstop, but he never barked; I would pet his head tenderly every time I saw a dog yelp from getting choked on its leash.

Only one dog was allowed out of the basement at a time. I never laid a hand on the other dogs, their powerful jaws frightening me. However, Bean

Boy didn't share my fear as he always wanted to play with them. The same dog that lunged at me that first day enjoyed chasing Bean Boy and me. It too had gray fur like Bean Boy, but he had patches of white on his face like a mask, and when he chased us, I feared it felt more like a hunt for him than play for us. I frequently scooped up Bean Boy and ran to my father for safety. That's why I called this dog Ruff – a fitting name I thought.

As Bean Boy and I slept in bed each night, we noticed a pattern. My father would leave the house with just one dog, with Bean Boy and I watching from the window above. We would fall asleep before they'd return, and after the first few times, I realized my father was in a good mood the next morning at the breakfast table. He would count up money as we ate, but as I shared my food with Bean Boy on my lap, my father's dogs were nowhere to be seen.

"Where's the dog you left with last night?" I finally asked.

My father didn't look me in the eye as he responded. "Resting downstairs. Let it be, Nikolai."

I never ventured downstairs; truthfully, I was scared of Ruff, and I believed he could rally all the dogs to bark at me if he wanted to. So, I took my father's word and let the dogs rest.

I was shocked awake one night to hear my father returning home. He shouted something and I heard him thunder upstairs. I heard him go into the spare room, slamming the door behind him. I kept my ear pressed to the door, too nervous to leave my room, and Bean Boy sniffed under my door. Suddenly I heard a dog cry out like I had never heard before. I grabbed Bean Boy and hid under the covers the rest of the night.

My father was not in a good mood the next morning, evident by his choice of beer for breakfast. I said nothing of what I heard, and shamefully I didn't look at my father, instead focusing on Bean Boy chewing with his mouth open.

Because of the rotation of dogs, it took a while for me to finally see that one of the dogs now only had three legs. It was moving slower and more cautiously now; stunningly, it was even scared by Bean Boy's naïve growl asking to play.

"What happened to his leg?" I asked.

"Wasn't a good leg. I did it a favor." Again, no eye contact. And foolishly, I let the matter go, too timid to risk my father's anger, and worse, too scared of his dogs to earnestly care for them.

Not just once. Not twice. But for every single one of my father's dogs, this pattern repeated.

And I didn't do a single damn thing about it.

✶✶✶✶✶

The Priority of the Orange Tree
Avery Johnston

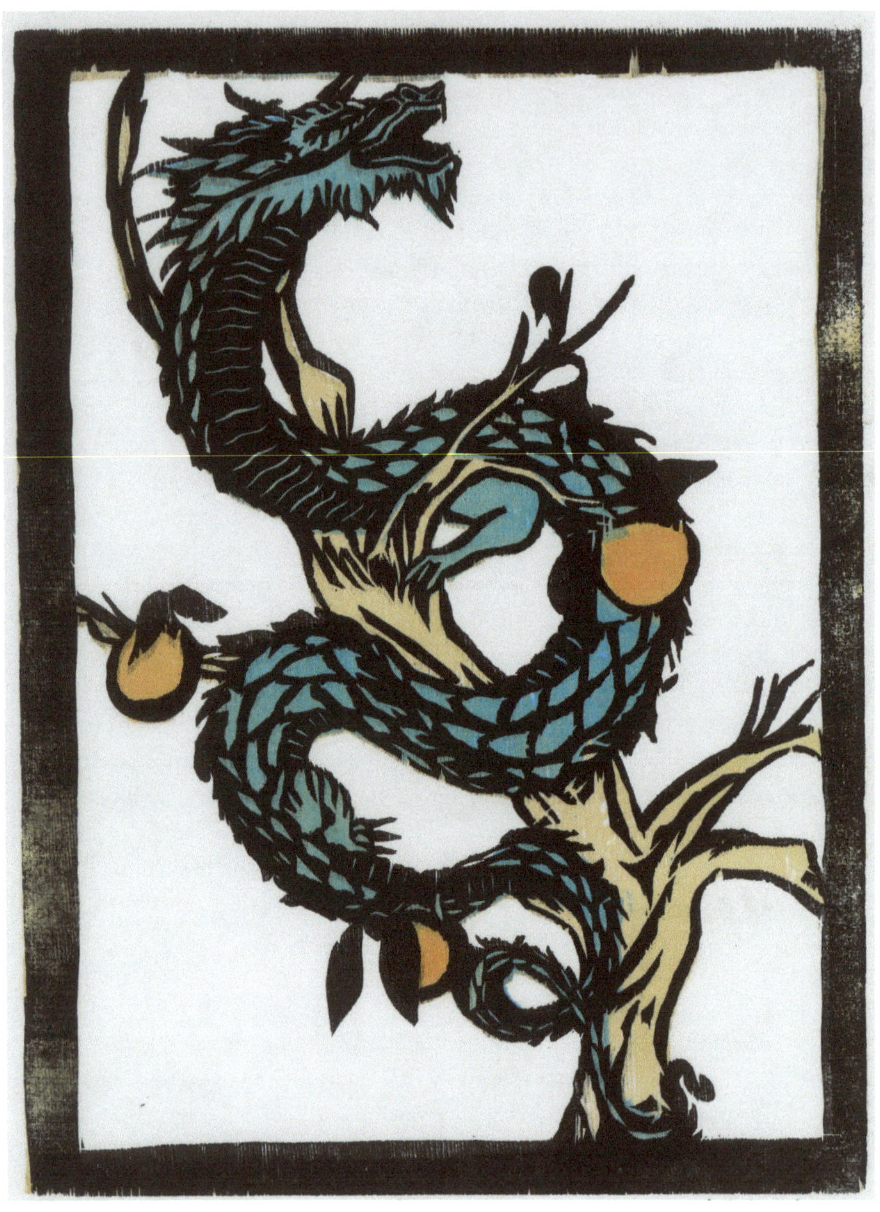

That night started like any other – Ruff was chasing Bean Boy and I again, his hobby unchanged even after losing a leg, but this time I ran upstairs to my room. I dared to peek back at Ruff, but he stopped chasing me when he reached the top of the stairs. With Bean Boy still in my arms, I cautiously walked back to see Ruff just standing there, staring at the spare room, eyes un-blinking. As I walked closer to the room, he became agitated, making growling noises, his single front paw starting to scratch the stairs. With a glance toward me, almost asking me not to open it, Ruff whined then ran away back down-stairs.

That was the last time I looked into Ruff's eyes while he was alive.

I turned around toward the door, with Bean Boy's attention now di-verted to it. His small tail beat against my chest, almost like a drum urging me on. It only now dawned on me that none of father's dogs ever came upstairs, and I decided to see why this room had the power to save me from Ruff. The door was heavy but unlocked, and with a push, it creaked open.

A dull light flickered from above, coming from a lamp dangling by a cord. Gone was the bed my mother must have drawn her last breath from; instead, a metal table dominated the middle of the room like an island. The smell of blood stung my nose, staining not only the floor around the table, but also the garden shears in the corner of the room. Rusted chains laid dormant next to the shears, and a large dirt covered trash can loomed in the corner. Bean Boy jumped out of my arms and ran toward the trash can, happily sniffing something there. I chased after him, but not before he grabbed a large bone in his mouth, longer than he was. I snatched it out of his mouth, leaving in a panic.

Safely in my room, under the covers with Bean Boy, I refused to think about the room. The ominous feeling could not leave me as I skipped dinner with Bean Boy, much to his disappointment. Before I knew it, night fell, with my father leaving with a dog again. I cuddled with Bean Boy, with him squeak-ing muffled barks in his sleep.

We heard my father return with a joyous exclamation in the kitchen. I forgot my fear of the room and went downstairs, Bean Boy following close. My father was drinking from a bottle with a large pile of money nearby. I didn't want to be around my father as he drank himself to sleep, so I turned away. As I headed back upstairs, I saw a figure through the window approach-ing the house. He seemed to be carrying something in his hands, covered in a dark blanket. I soon recognized him as the stranger from months ago, Sergei.

He let himself in the door as my father failed to lock it behind him. He towered above me with a grim expression on his face. Bean Boy went to go stand up against his leg, trying in vain to lick his face.

Sergei looked down upon me and spoke. "Tell your father not to leave his fuckin' mess behind," he said, dropping what he was holding.

It was Ruff. He hit the floor with a dull thud. He was covered in blood and gashes, his white mask ruined.

"Wh- wh- what-" I stammered.

"Finally got his fucking payoff. We all thought it was a gimmick at first, Pyotr and his little crippled underdogs. But all it took was a bunch of out of towners to fall for the trick and bet high against the son of a bitch. Good for Pyotr," he spat without an ounce of affection. And with that he turned and left into the night.

I fell to my knees next to Ruff and saw he was still breathing. And from there I just stopped moving. I sat there for at least half an hour, listening to the dog wheeze, my mind flashing back to the sounds of my mother behind the door. At some point, Bean Boy understood that his "brother" was not moving or responding to his attempts to play, and the puppy began licking Ruff's face.

How naïve! How fucking naïve I was! On some level I always knew my father was hurting the dogs in some way, and now I knew that room was clearly connected to them losing a leg. But I thought – no I hoped – that my father and his dogs could remain in a separate sphere from Bean Boy and I, that I was allowed my own life and happiness. However, now, with Ruff dead in front of me, I realized every single dog in this house was at the mercy of my father, and I knew I had to do something about it.

I dashed down the basement stairs and opened the basement door leading to the backyard, the dark woods visible from the house. My heart was thrashing against my chest as I fumbled the nearby key toward the lock, the last step almost complete. And with a sudden click and swing, the large cage was open.

"Go!" I shouted, my adrenaline giving me the authority to command them. Without hesitation, they all rose on their three legs and bolted out of the house, heading straight for the woods.

But… how careless… Bean Boy with me the whole time, and in his excitement, he chased after his brothers. I ran helplessly after him as Bean Boy's wagging tail moved further and further away from me than he had ever been.

But Bean Boy's love for me pulled through as he turned around to look at me. I could feel myself about to call for him, but the house exerted its dark pressure on me. If Bean Boy was to stay with me, how could I possibly prevent my father from turning him into his next fighter? If I was naïve before by ignoring the dog fighting, then how could I let myself be naïve again and assume my father thought Bean Boy was off limits?

The tears came instantly, and instead of calling for Bean Boy to come back, I shouted "Go!" – or at least I tried to. I couldn't bring myself to say such a thing, and all that left through my sobbing was a hoarse whisper. Bean Boy looked at me for the final time, tail still wagging, and then he followed after his brothers into the darkness.

That was the last time I felt loved.

Considering why I'm writing this to begin with, it should come as no surprise that my father did not take kindly to my action that night. As soon as my father found out and grabbed me in a rage, I lost all hope of growing up decently. Through my tears and shouting, through his drunken fury, as he dragged me upstairs, I was losing the only hope of being someone else, someone who wouldn't grow up to mutilate his father into pieces.

My father simply wanted to do me a favor. To make me stronger. Now, when you see me in person, with the eyes of a killer and my own leg missing, maybe you agree and consider me stronger. On that night, my father knew of no better way to force the weakness out.

And so, my father took me into the room the dogs were scared of.

The Study of Sisyphus
Giselle Ramos

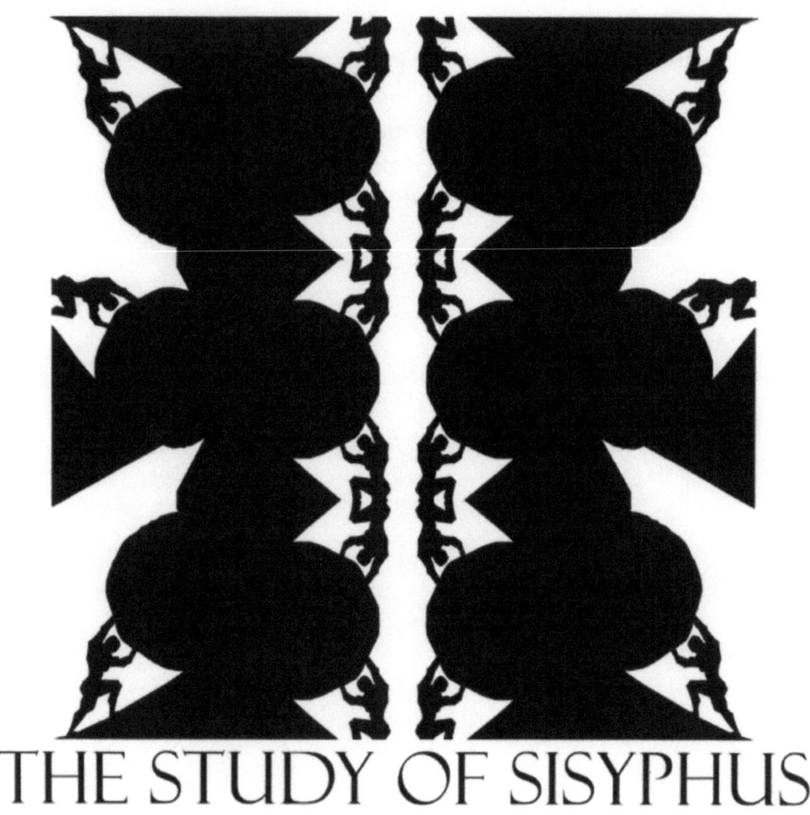

Hell in Doses
Reed Reilly

Three men stood next to each other facing the large mountain that sloped upward to a swept peak. They were in a large plain that was made wet by an afternoon drizzle. Tall, brass grass flanked the group. It was weighed down slightly by the rain but jumped delicately in the wind. Not a tree was in sight. At the peak of the slope, a shard of stone jutted skyward with an enormous crooked-necked bird preening under its wing resting atop it. It was filthy black and had a bald cap on its head. Despite the ugly nature of the beast, it had smooth, dense, intricate feathering that covered all but the summit of its body just as the mountain was covered with dirt and greenery except for the stone protrusion. The men's vision moved from the bird down the rocky, steep mountain face and toward the massive, smooth boulder. They stood gazing at it, as if they were leering at a woman's bare legs, for quite some time.

"What is it?" said the round, short man on the left.

"Syphilis's boulder," said the giant, rude looking man on the right.

"Sisyphus's boulder," said the medium height slim man between them.

"Whatever," said the giant. "We're supposed to roll it to the top?"

"Presumably," said the slim man.

"It's gotta be impossible, though," chirped the short man.

They all looked up to the mountain face for another while. They all seemed to be in agreement that it was a fool's task, but their hope had not faded entirely. Their dull eyes caressed the smooth, round stone that stood before them. It reminded the giant of a granite cueball.

"We're gonna get it up there," said the slim man under his breath. But the others understood. He and the giant took steps forward, while the short man followed, stumbling slightly.

They pushed. It rolled easily along the wet grass until it met the first curve of the hill. They strained and it raised. The three pushed and shoved the mass another thirty feet up the slope before the short man slipped on a piece of wet grass and the other two lost their grip on the damp surface. It slid from their grasps, and it glided downward before resting in the same place they had found it. "Goddammit," huffed the giant through heavy breaths. They all rested their hands on their knees and panted.

The slim man was smiling. "It bleeds," he whispered.

The trio spent a long time hauling the object up in an attempt to reach the pinnacle. It never reached, but they got far. One evening, as the three sat at the base of the hill, each leaning on the rock in the same pattern they arrived in, they changed their strategy. They would dig trenches at intervals up the face so that they could stow the boulder and recover their strength. In the morning, they began on the first checkpoint. Their fingers bled after clawing at the ground for only a few minutes. The short man wanted to take a break, but he was fearful of the hateful gazes he was sure to receive from the other men. They all dug until bones began to show, because they all secretly held the same fear as the short man. The progress they had made was paltry, they had hardly made a dent. Still, there was hope deep in the eyes of the men. On the slim man, you wouldn't even have to look that deeply.

One day, after a day prior of grueling digging and bloody phalanges, the giant proposed another idea.

"Why do we even push it? Would our lives not be easier if we just sat down here and basked in the sun, instead of sweating in it? Wouldn't it be better if we showered in the rain instead of working in it? Why the hell do we do it?" The day was a fine one. They would rest on good days like this, which they called "Sundays." They were rare.

"I suppose it's a better purpose than doing nothing," said the slim man. "That's why we do it. We just forgot. There's also the chance that if we get the damned rock up the hill it might…"

"Don't fucking jinx it!" shouted the giant. "We've gone this long, don't jinx it."

"What does it matter," said the short man. He was weary. "I would be happier to just sit in mud than go back up that hill. And it don't matter if we jinx it or not, we ain't leaving here. Syssyfits didn't escape, did he?"

The other two wanted to renounce the short man's theories, but they relented and resigned. They did not work that day, or the next. They spent many days lying about, not touching the stone nor the mountain even once. As the days went on, however, the weather worsened. Where there were once only days heavy with rain and ones heavy with heat, now the days were burdened with both. Storms that turned the field into a murky sea and droughts that made their lips crack and their skin taut. There were fewer and fewer Sundays as the dreary weather continued. Finally, on a day thick with clouds and deep with rain, the men sat deep-set in wet dirt and itchy grass, a conversation struck up.

"I want to get back to work," said the slim man, "and I think you all should too.

"What?" asked the short man, "why the hell would you say something like that?"

"For two reasons. One: because the weather is obviously getting worse in response to our sloth." He motioned around their heads. "Look around and tell me that it was ever even close to this bad when we were hauling. Two: I am less happy sitting in this mud than I was moving the rock. Grueling labor and fingers worn to the bone are more appealing to me than pointless misery."

"Rolling the boulder is misery, though," said the giant.

"But not pointless misery," said the slim man. "In fact, I would go so far as to call it purposeful misery, even."

"It is pointless." snarled the short man. "What fucking purpose is there to roll that stupid rock up that stupid hill? What makes that a better purpose than my purpose, rolling in this wet, muddy grass until the end of time?"

"Your purpose, sir," said the slim man, "is garbage. How do you define a successful day rolling in the mud like the fat pig you are? When you've successfully coated your rotund body in three greasy layers of grime?"

"The only pig here is you!" yelled the short man. "You're a fuckin' capitalist pig, is what you are. You want us all to work and work and work for nothing. Let me tell you something, sir, work ain't no purpose. It ain't no purpose at all."

"You are incorrect in your belief from top to bottom. There can be purpose. It's not the best, and it's not the one I'd pick to spend a million years pursuing, but it is one. Believe me, if I could find a pen and paper in this field or on that mountain, I'd make it my purpose to spend every day writing love letters to Maggie, but there isn't even a tree to mill."

"Maggie?" asked the giant.

"Don't worry about that. Haven't either of you ever found purpose in your work, even a little? Ever?"

There were a few seconds of silence.

"When I was a gardener," the giant said softly.

"Yes!" said the slim man. "And was that the best purpose that you've ever had?

"Hell no. That'd be raising my daughters, easily."

"But there was something, wasn't th…"

"Do you even hear yourself right now?" yelled the short man. "You two want to haul a boulder up that hill forever? Even if something happened once it got up there, which it won't, I'd rather watch the grass grow and the flies die than touch that sick piece of granite one more time! I'd rather melt into the earth than get one more blister digging those trenches. As a matter of fact, I don't think I'd push that boulder up even if Jesus Christ himself came to pat me on the back and take me to heaven after."

Many moments of angry air followed the short man's monologue.

"I thought you were Jewish," said the giant.

More moments passed.

"I'm getting back to work," the slim man sighed. He knew that the giant would follow shortly, and that one day even the short man would rejoin them. It was only a matter of time.

Pouring Iron
Terry Quill

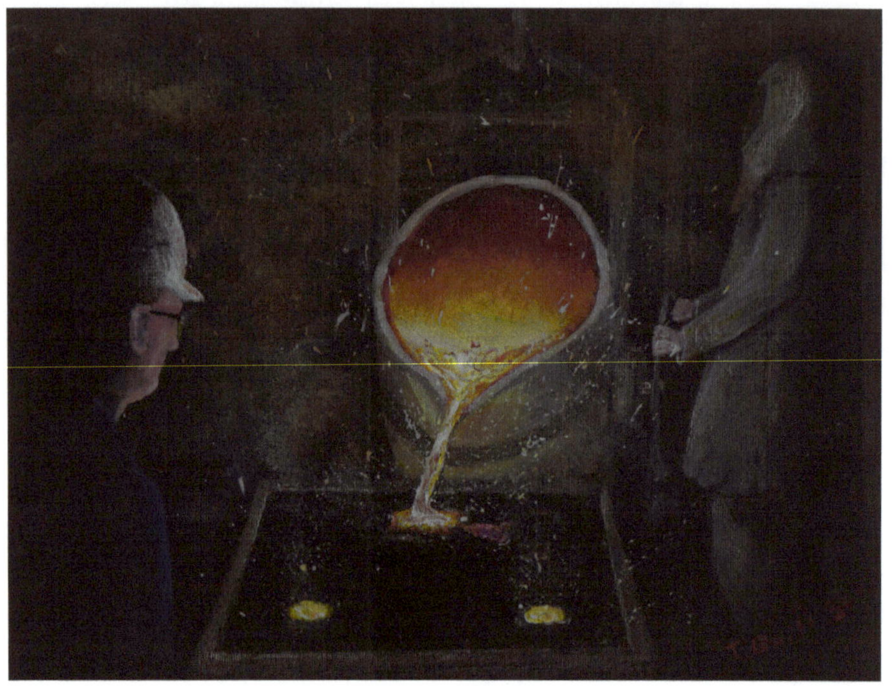

*****

For scores of years, the men dug. They dug and they planned, and they practiced, and explored the world they found themselves in. They were each looking for clues, of which they each found none. They were in no doubt as to where they were, and as to why they were there for that matter, but they didn't understand much else about their circumstances. It would always stay that way.

But they did inch further. They had now been rolling the boulder for longer than the oldest of them, the slim man, had been on earth. It was a strange sensation for them to recall memories from so long ago when they would talk as they dug and rolled. They discovered that they were all there for the same reason; they each did more bad than good. No single condemning sin, but lifetimes of carelessness. They lamented their wasted lives each day, and sometimes the regret clutched their hearts like talons, but they tried not to let the others catch on. They could get the boulder far up the mountain with little effort now. It was amusing to them to see it set so high near the crest. Relatively near, but they were close.

One day, after many lifetimes of digging and hauling and aching, the men knew their task was coming to an end. Trenches were dug all the way up the mountain, they had practiced endlessly, and not a single measure could be thought of that they had not taken in ensuring that they were successful in their task. They got to work. They rolled the boulder up to the first trench, sixty feet up the hill, and rested for the remainder of the day. Each day, with nerves and excitement sloshing in each of their chests, they would make it one trench closer to the summit. The uneasy excitement of butterflies found in each of the three reminded them of moments of similar magnitude in their lives. When the slim man would see Maggie after a great expanse of time, when the giant witnessed each of his daughters born, and when the short man would receive his first piece of cherry cobbler each Thanksgiving as a boy.

The final day of the climb, there were many Maggies, daughters, and cherry cobblers to be had at the top. The men left the final stretch longest, knowing excitement would carry them the extra distance. On that final day, each man's arms and legs tore from stain, their hearts were on the verge of bursting, and their lungs wore as thin as sandwich bags, but they got the stone to the top.

The boulder came to rest in a divot just the right size to hold it. It sat firmly. The three men looked at it with shattered expressions. The giant began to weep. He began to sob. Snot and tears and sweat soaked his face. The short man started soon after. The two of them bawled with elation and wiped endless goo from their faces with their wrists. The slim man stood, still in disbelief. He looked at the rock with a funny expression. It caught up to him, and he joined the other two in making tears.

*****

After some minutes, the boulder rose from the divot and rolled down the mountain until it came to rest below the clouds and near where the men discovered it for the first time. The earth shook the men to their backs and when they stood, the trenches had smoothed over.

"What?" the giant asked, thirsting for knowledge. "What the hell was that?" The high had not left him, though he was confused.

The slim man was still smiling the same as before. "It doesn't matter, man. We did it." His breath quaked with excitement.

"W-what do you mean it doesn't matter?" groaned the short man. "It's all gone, and we've got nothing to show for it. The trenches closed up. We're just back where we started 300 years ago or however-the-fuck-long we've been here! I told you it was for nothing!"

"You don't understand," the slim man said sternly, still smirking. "We. Did. It." He enunciated every word. "And that's assuming you were correct in your assumption, which you are not. Look." He gestured toward the massive bird a few feet from them. A single, small black feather lay at the base of its perch.

"Do you think…" started the giant.

"Yes," said the slim man, 'I do, and we're gonna stay here until that bird is as plucked as a Christmas chicken. And after that, I have reason to believe something new will happen. I hope that's our exodus from this place."

"You hope?" asked the short man.

"I do. And I believe it, too. At the very least, something comes after this hill. I don't know what, you've got me there, but set aside your pessimism for five minutes and enjoy our victory."

"But…" The giant's face was bubbling with tears again. "But that means we're not even close to done yet. There's gotta be thousands of feathers on that bird."

The slim man walked over to the fallen feather and picked it up. He moved towards the giant, placed it in his hand, and closed five massive fingers around it.

"But there is an end, brother. If not after this burden, then the next. We will know rest one day; I promise you that. Nothing can last forever. No heaven, no god, and no hell. We will leave this place, one feather at a time." He turned to the short man. "You are right, my friend, there is often no pleasure in our lives, but there will be an end. We will take our hell one day at a time, one second at a time if we need to. Now please, both of you, rest with me on this crest. We will have much to do tomorrow."

Waiting with Art Bags
Xin Ray Penland Obrien

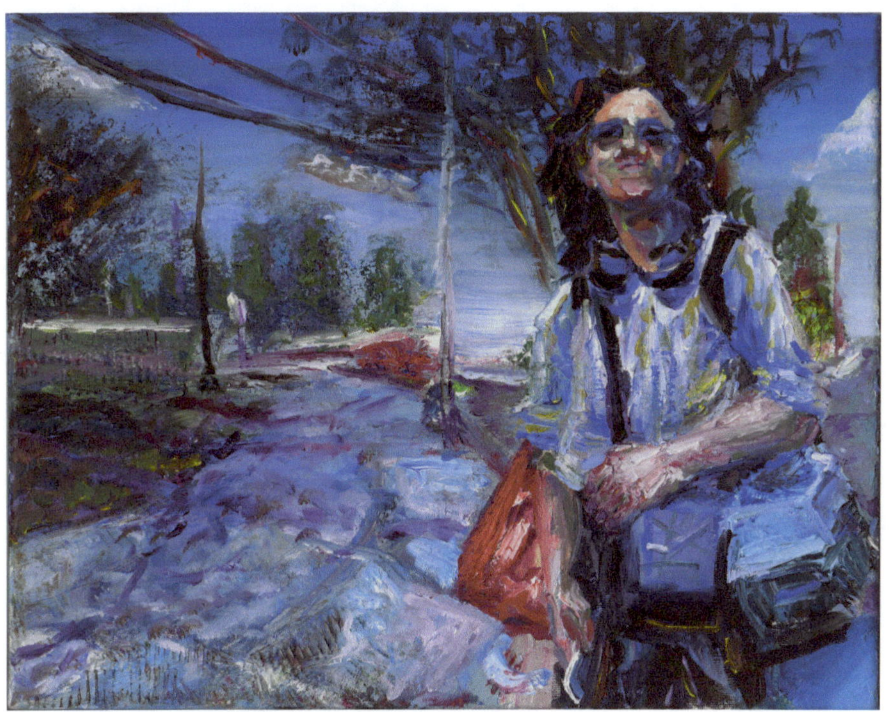

Schism
Nicolette Israel

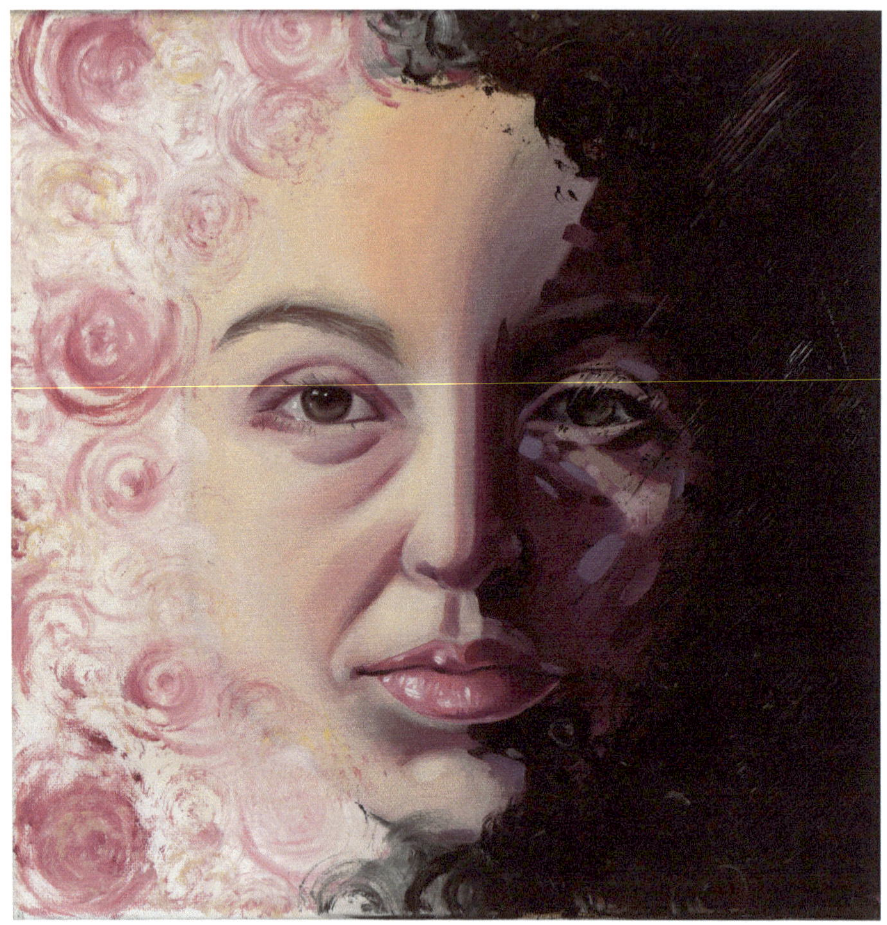

Stay
Ilana Maiman

Martinez wakes up in a cocoon of warmth. Not only is she nestled under five blankets, a quilt, and a heavy-duty comforter, she's also got a big muscular arm keeping her close to a big muscular chest. It's a moment she wishes she could stay in forever; quit her life of international espionage and just live in a breathless moment between sleep and waking.

She shakes the thought from her mind, pushing herself from the cocoon and into the cold winter morning of the St. Petersburg safe house. She begins to gather various clothing items and weapons from around the room. Grant's still asleep, the peaceful lull of his breathing drawing her heart back to bed like the tide. She considers staying in Grant's bulky arms.

She sighs, shaking her head. She walks to the front door and steps outside without another glance at Grant.

It's snowing in St. Petersburg. The wind whips at Martinez's face as she sneaks down the alley away from Grant and the safehouse. She tucks her chin in towards her chest and flips the lapels of her coat up around her face. This is the part that she's used to: the leaving.

It's necessary for their jobs, of course. She might be on Grant's team but the spy life was a solo one, and it was usually safer to report remotely than in person. She and Grant only had these little dalliances when they needed to team up properly. She shouldn't—she won't—get too attached.

Damn Grant, with his bright blue eyes that can see a whole world beyond the one they're in. He's crazy. He makes her feel alive.

She feels a tug in her chest, knowing how long it will be until she sees him again. She buries it somewhere deep in the snow under her feet.

*****

The first time Grant sees Martinez, the world stops short.

She's unremarkable to him at first. Sure, she's pretty; her big brown eyes and sleek black ponytail, all complemented beautifully by her olive skin. But she's just another agent in a long line of them that Grant's training with. He doesn't really see her until they're paired together to spar. Grant is 6'3, which means he's gotta have at least a foot on Martinez. And that's not to mention his muscles, which might as well be the size of his head.

She takes him in, brown eyes flitting over every inch of him, sizing him up. Her brow furrows. Her bottom lip tucks between her top and bottom teeth. For a second, he thinks she's afraid to fight him. But then he watches her, all that fear on her face rippling like he'd touched the surface of water and then settling and smoothing out into something determined.

"You ready?" She asks him. He nods, thinking the fight will be over before he knows it.

It is. Martinez has him flat on his back in less than 30 seconds, the determination he'd seen cracking into a smug smirk.

He's gone on her from that moment on.

*****

Martinez stumbles through the door of the St. Petersburg safehouse around midnight, tipsy and in the middle of smudging her lipstick all over Grant's face. They're only a few steps in the doorway before they're shedding their clothes. They're lucky the place is just a studio apartment. Otherwise, they wouldn't make it to the bed.

It's become a routine for her and Grant to do this; go out, get drinks, and hook up when they're on assignment together. Martinez didn't have any illusions that it was something serious. They didn't fall into bed with each other because they fell in love; they fell into bed with each other because they're each other's only option. They weren't exactly in a business that begot trust. Martinez is available for Grant. She's easy.

And yet...

Clifton Grant touches her like she's precious. He brings her to climax and then clings to her like she's the answer he's been searching for. He traces gentle patterns into her bare hip in the aftermath, while her mind is occupied with exit strategies.

"You gonna be here when I wake up?" he whispers when he thinks she's asleep.

No, she says to herself. She lives to disappoint.

*****

Grant has a backpack. He calls it a "knapsack" and Martinez teases him for it every time.

From what she's observed, it contains a few changes of clothes, a little notebook, a compass, a case full of pencils, and a sketchbook. She sees him sketching in it all the time, although she never quite catches what he's drawing. But she wonders. And he leaves his backpack on the floor when he takes her to bed.

She wakes up in the middle of the night one night, while they're staying at a Motel Six in Reno. The backpack is sitting on the floor across the room, staring at her.

She tiptoes over to the bag, careful not to wake Grant. She rifles through it until she feels the leather spine of the sketchbook and grabs on for dear life, running on tiptoe over to the hotel room bathroom. She sits on the toilet seat and opens the book.

Grant is remarkably good. He's got some landscapes from different missions; the wintery outline of St. Petersburg makes Martinez smile. There's some familiar faces, Wilson and Remington, two agents Martinez knows professionally who Grant considers friends. There are a couple sketches of Martinez, one of her back that must've been done one night while she slept, or her silhouette mid-fight that must've been done from memory.

Judging how often she saw Grant drawing she'd assumed he'd have to have sketched her at some point. It's not surprising; she's there. She lingers on the silhouette for a moment before flipping the page.

It takes her breath away. It's her again, but unlike any of the others. In this one she's smiling; head tilted over to one side, lips pursed from the effort of keeping in a full-on laugh. Her eyes twinkle.

Martinez stands quickly, looking into the bathroom mirror. She smiles. She frowns.

She has all the same features as the woman from the sketch; same hair and eyes and nose.

But she can't recreate that twinkle. It's not an expression she can bring out of herself, she realizes. It's an expression only he can.

She quickly shuts the bathroom light, returns the sketchbook to Grant's backpack, and crawls back into bed.

*****

Grant's on a highway in the middle of Middle America, driving a beige Honda Odyssey that smells like the ghost of youth soccer game orange slices. Martinez sits on the passenger's side with her boots up on the dash (an argument he'd long since given up on). They've been talking to pass the time.

"So how'd you get into the business?" he asks, his tone light.

Martinez shrugs in the passenger's seat. "My parents died when I was a teen, and I got into being angry, beating people up. I got into a really bad fight with a neighbor's shitty boyfriend. Cops were called, he succumbed to the injuries. But my case worker saw potential I guess. The agency recruited me from there."

"Wow," Grant whistles a little, "that's—"

"Fucked up?"

He shakes his head. "I was gonna say brave." Beside him, Martinez snorts.

He frowns. "I'm serious."

Martinez's dark eyes find Grant's and force goosebumps on his arms with their severity. "When you recruited me, you said this could turn into the fight of my life."

There's this awful expression on her face that Grant recognizes from his military days but can't quite name.

"I wasn't noble," Martinez says to his forehead. "I was hungry."

*****

It'd be wrong to tell her she's beautiful right then, but he thinks it.

*****

There's dirt all over Martinez's body, seeping into her pores and her lungs and somehow, her heart. She's on her back in the middle of a warehouse they've just raided. Her ribs burn, and without any examination she's pretty sure there's internal bleeding. And also a knife wound.

The comms in her ears crackle to life. Grant's voice comes out over the static. "Martinez? You good? "

Martinez tries to sit up and tell Grant she's alright at the same time, but all that comes out is a cry of pain.

"Martinez?!"

She sucks a breath through her teeth, biting back a scream. Her ribs burn so much that disembowelment seems like a better option than struggling her way back to the jet. Grant calls for her over the comms, but it takes a second for her hearing to get back online.

"Martinez?!! Where are you? Ximena?!!"

"I'm here, Grant. It's gonna—shit—take me a second to get to you."

"Don't even think about it, I'm coming to you."

Martinez doesn't know how long she lies there. Eventually she hears the familiar clomp of Grant's boots, getting faster and louder when he spots her on the ground.

There's a moment where he just stands there, stunned and frankly quite useless, looking her over. He tilts his head at her, arms held out on either side, eyes raking over her weakened frame.

"I don't want to hurt you," he says at last.

Martinez chuckles through gritted teeth, and almost blacks out from the pain it sends through her ribs.

"Don't know if that's an option."

Self-Portrait
Alexander Beaudreau

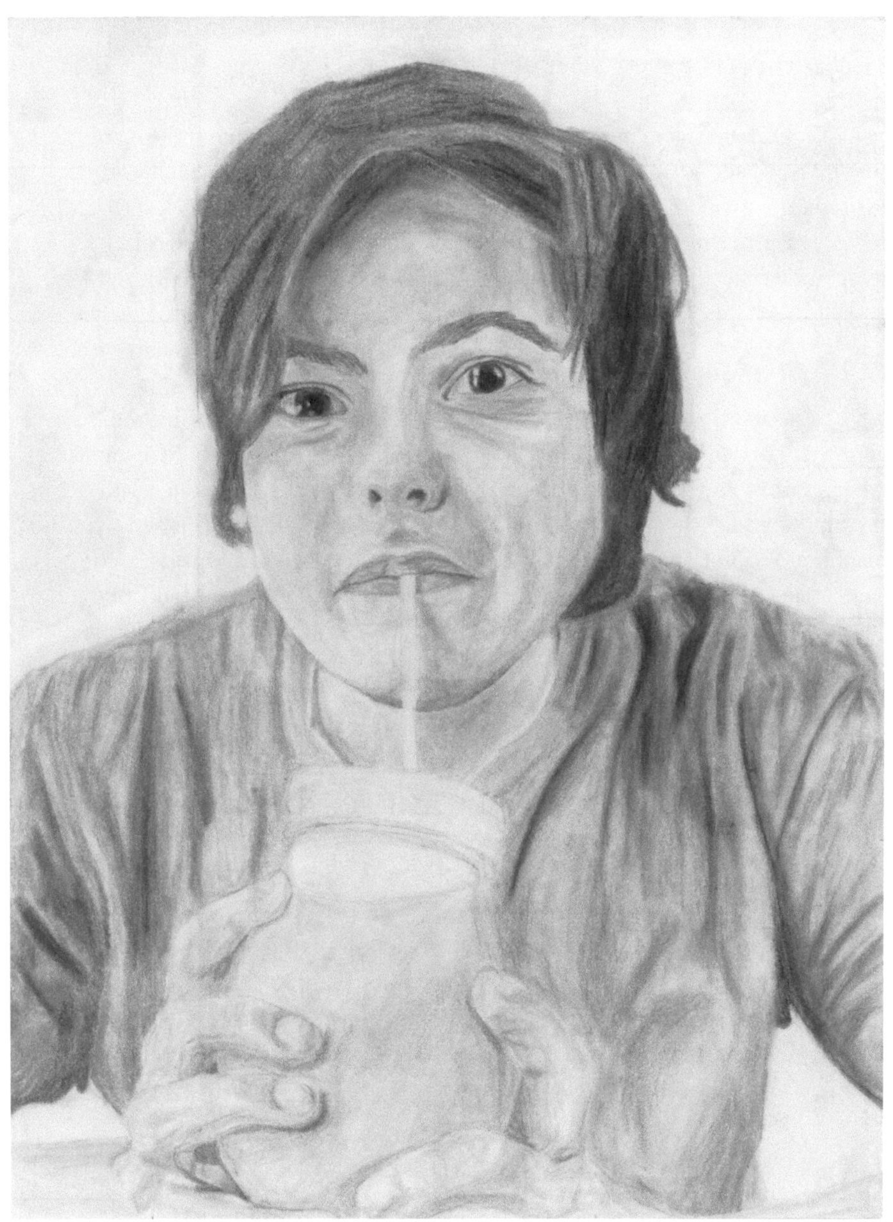

He nods, looking a bit sheepish. As gently as he can manage, he eases Martinez into his arms, taking extra care around her bloody rib cage. The whole affair takes about five minutes, but she manages to find a position in his arms.

She knows she needs to stay awake, but her eyelids have a different agenda. They close every other second, heavy and getting increasingly hard to fight.

"Ximena, you still with me?" Grant asks, panic rising in his tone. "Unfortunately," she says, forcing her eyelids open just in time to catch Grant's expression.

Damn him, he smiles at that. And damn her, she bares her bloody teeth and smiles back.

*****

Martinez wakes up in a motel room. It's the sleazy rent-by-the hour variety: a parking lot right in front of the rooms, half a century of cigarette stench poorly masked with citrus and bleach, a vibrating bed advertised on the nightstand. A handwritten sign reads "OUT OF ORDER" taped over the machine. Wood paneling lines the wall behind the two double beds, a contrast against a carpet that can diplomatically be described as "once bright orange."

"Can I get you anything?" Grant asks from the double bed opposite hers. He's giving his best impression of a concerned mother. Martinez smiles a little at that. Grant's brow furrows.

"What?"

"You make a good nurse," she tells him.

"Yeah?" He walks over and sits down next to her on the bed, feet ghosting over the ugly orange carpet.

"My mom was a nurse," his smile is shy and wistful.

"Well, I think you'd make her proud."

Martinez means it as a joke, but the words fall from her lips too softly.

There's something achingly close about Grant right now. She's been naked in front of him in bed before, but she's never felt so exposed with him. Grant seems to pick up on it as well. He drops his gaze to his hands.

"You almost died," he all but whispers. Martinez swallows.

"I did."

Grant nods. His eyebrows knit together in that way they do when he's preparing for a fight.

Grant says, "Melina thinks I'm in love with you..." Melina's always right about people, Martinez thinks. "...but I think you already knew that."

Maybe Grant's right about people too.

"Yeah," Martinez breathes. "I know."

Grant searches Martinez's face for a sign, the way he'd done in a thousand moments before this one. She has no words.

"Right," he coughs, nodding to himself. "Well, I'll, ah, go then."

He moves to stand from the bed, legs sliding across the bedding, feet hovering over the floor. Martinez's hand darts out to grab his.

"Dammit, Cliff," she pulls his face down towards hers and kisses him.

Kissing Grant feels like climbing a tree as a child. It feels like sunlight on Martinez's face. It feels like everything she never had; safety and warmth and arms that reach for her only to offer comfort.

Grant brings his arms up around her, and he feels like he's holding the whole world. He's always been Atlas with the world on his shoulders. But now he's discovering that when the world shifts from his shoulders to his arms and takes Martinez's shape, its weight is bearable. Its weight is glorious.

The kissing goes on for a while, slow and soft and achingly tender in that way Grant is with her. She pulls away only when she thinks it might kill her.

"This isn't easy for me," she whispers to him.

"Shh," Grant smooths hair away from her eyes. "We can talk tomorrow. Right now just be here."

Martinez sighs. Her stomach clenches at the mere thought of staying the night but there isn't much she can do bed-bound as she is. Besides, she's tired of trying to convince Grant not to love her.

"Okay," she agrees, letting Grant help ease her down under the covers. She falls asleep in the warmth of motel blankets and Grant's arms.

*****

Grant blinks sleep from his eyes. Pale sunlight leaks through the gap in the beige motel curtains, tinting the garishly warm-toned motel room into something almost serene. He tries to bring his left hand up to wipe at his eye, only to find something heavy blocking his way. He looks down.

Martinez's long dark hair lays out across the pillow next to him, askew where her normally sleek ponytail had fallen out in her sleep. Grant's eyes widen, taking in the peaceful expression on her sleeping face, the way her long eyelashes gently rest against her closed eyes.

Grant can't help himself from grinning so wide it nearly splits his cheeks. He lays back down and pulls Martinez closer into his chest, tucking her head under his chin. He closes his eyes and drifts back to sleep.

Sweet Gum Leaves
Mary Ott

58

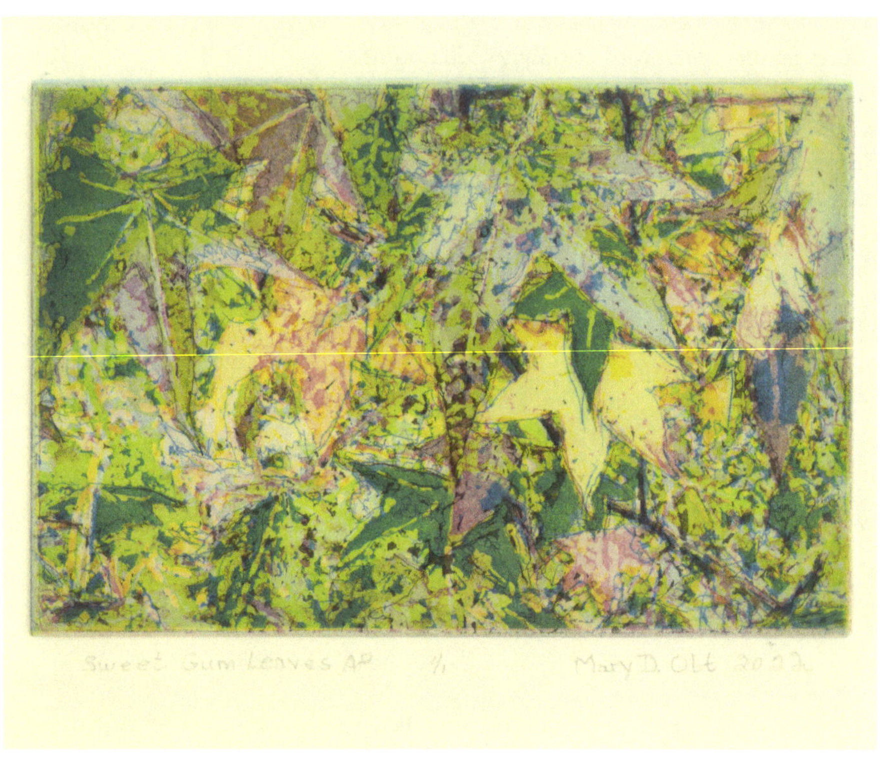

Emergency Contact
Alexandra Bouvier

I'm sitting in the car. From the outside looking in everything seems normal, but the air is laced with a thick tension. It makes sense considering where I've just been picked up from and where I'm heading now. A phantom tug of complete and utter exhaustion comes over me as I try to come to terms with what's to come.

My mother is pulling away from the specialty clinic she just picked me up from. My doctor didn't really give me much of a choice. It was either to have an ambulance be called or have my mother immediately drive me to the ER. I chose the lesser of the two evils. My doctor tried to explain the severity of the situation. He explained I looked pale and lifeless. Fragile almost. He held my hands with a careful tenderness I didn't realize I'd been craving. He said my hands were too cold, though I looked at the translucent purple shade of my hands with indifference. He also said I needed IV resuscitation. Electrolytes, saline, and possibly dextrose. I needed more advanced resources to check the state of my organs than just the stethoscope around his neck and the portable vitals machine in the clinic's office. Honestly, I heard this all before, one too many times, so I didn't think much of it. Regardless, I dug around for my phone in my jacket pocket and pressed on the name I'd done so many times before. She's my mother. My emergency contact of sorts. I'm always swept away by that natural instinct that comes with being the daughter or son of a mother. She's supposed to be there for anything. Love me through anything.

"Mom." I cleared my throat into my phone. "He said I need to go to the hospital. I have to be admitted. And… I can't go alone. I need you to drive me. Please."

And she came right away to pick me up. Her annoyance and reluctance seeped through the phone, coating me in its uncomfortable stickiness. Quietly labeling me a burden.

*****

As my mother and I drive in silence, my mind wanders to the events of last evening. The utter depravity of what happened has yet to sink in until now. I have been staying at my grandma's apartment. Unfortunately, my grandma's not-so-watchful gaze allowed me to fester in my illness. She asked me to walk her dog that evening. I had already been lying on the pullout bed in her living room, attempting to ease the pain of my body seemingly decomposing while I was still alive. At least that's what it felt like. My grandma reminded me to walk the dog, so I gathered myself up the best I could. I leashed the dog, trudged to the elevator, and made my journey to the overused patch of grass outside of the building near the barely used back entrance. As I, and that bystander of a dog, decided to make our way back inside, I felt the most nauseating wave of pain wash over me. My legs gave out and black dots danced in front of my eyes. It was the telltale sign I was near passing out. However, for the first time ever I did not regain my vision almost immediately. Instead, I pathetically fought my way back inside the building, with a dog in tow, to the elevator, and back up to the 9th floor. All while essentially blind. Though I recovered my eyesight when I returned to bed, my mind was in a state of shock. How mortifying it would have been if someone had seen me crawling back to the apartment door. What other 20-year-old spends their Tuesday evening embarrassingly incapacitated due to their own idiocy. *Though I can't really help what's happening to me. It's not on purpose. Well... my mother would beg to differ.*

I'm so pathetic.

*****

I try to get more comfortable in the passenger seat of the car, as discretely as I can. I don't want to draw attention to myself. I can't help but react like I'm some sort of domestic abuse victim, afraid to make a move, but that's how it's playing out. I lower the seat and take laboring breaths, as my muscles and bones feel as if they are eating themselves, and my heart feels as if someone is angrily squeezing it. One wrong move and I wholeheartedly believe my bones will crumble to dust beneath me. I internally chide myself for letting a pained moan slip out.

"What is wrong with you?!" my mother seethes, giving me a disparaging look. I shudder at the venom she spits into her words.

What's wrong with me?? That's rich. She's not driving me to the ER for shits and giggles. But I can't say that out loud. God, why did she have to say it like that? I can't help what's happening.

"I just don't feel very well," I placate with a whisper. Knowing her, she probably thinks I'm purposely in a bad mood. "I'm not upset, I... I... I'm just trying to rest for a second." My hidden pleas for her compassion fall on deaf ears though. "I'm okay," I gulp.

And as she yells, "God, I don't even know what to do with you anymore! Why are you doing this to yourself!" with zero empathy folded in.

I'm suddenly back in our tiny hallway on the second story of our house, sprawled out on the floor. I'm gathering my bearings as I realize I just passed out, taking up the little space that connects the four upstairs bedrooms. I see a figure starting its descent down the stairs that wasn't there when I first walked out into the hallway.

"Matthew!" the figure calls. "She passed out again."

I wait on the floor, but no one comes.

I feel dirty, problematic, and embarrassed.

And only later did I realize that that figure was my mother. She had been in her room. And as she came across my seemingly lifeless body on the hallway floor, she made the decision to step over me and continue down the stairs. No one checked in on me. But all I can remember is feeling awful as if I did something wrong. And I skate over the fact that I had just been blatantly neglected.

A horn blares nearby, shocking me out of my trance. Bringing me back to the present. I feel surprised at the wetness on my cheeks, but it's okay. I'm sure my mother won't notice. More tears spill from my eyes, my mouth opening and closing a few times pointlessly.

I resign myself to staring listlessly out the window.

"It's okay, mom, I'm okay." I try to cling to the fact that I so desperately want her love. She's loved me before. I know she has.

I can remember an evening almost a month ago. It was very late at night, and I had been in a deep state of sleep. I felt an odd pressure on the top of my foot, that went away quickly after. "Wh…what? Hello?" I croaked. There was no response. Just gentle shushing. Only the morning after did I realize that it was my mother in my room. She had been checking if I had a pulse. She wanted to know if I was alive.

I naively cling to that memory. Please love me, please love me, please love me. I chant in my head.

"Anna," my mother interrupts my thoughts, "get a grip."

Oh, okay.

"Yes, mom," I murmur.

*****

Lost in my thoughts, I almost miss the fact that we've arrived at the hospital. I can't help but feel a wave of unease as I realize she didn't park in the hospital parking lot. No, she pulled up outside the emergency room. Oh God. She's leaving me here. She's not coming with me.

She *always* comes with me.

"Well, we're here," she snaps. My brows furrow as I detect a hint of anxiety in her voice.

"Mom," I try, "are you not coming in with me?" I sigh, rolling my head to look out the passenger window. "I'm not sure with my bags if I can… you know." But I don't finish that thought. I don't think she'd be happy to hear that I don't think I can make it all the way to triage without collapsing.

Giving Story
Niamh Ducey

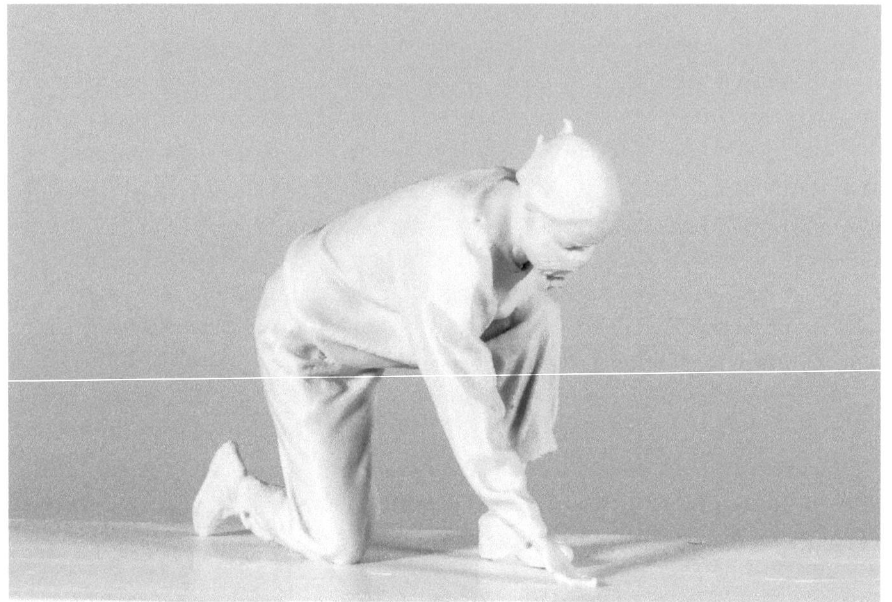

She doesn't say anything in reply. It's almost as if she can finally be done. Wash her hands of me. She doesn't want to draw this out any further.

I can't help but think of one of my favorite childhood stories. *The Runaway Bunny* by Margaret Wise Brown. The first line in the story is like sticky tack to the front of my brain.

Once there was a little bunny who wanted to run away. So he said to his mother, "I am running away."

"If you run away," said his mother, "I will run after you. For you are my little bunny."

Through the haze in my mind, I can't help but want her to tell me that I am her little bunny. That she'll follow me anywhere. That I will always have her heart to come back to. But I don't hear it.

I dejectedly reach for the door handle. Accepting my bleak fate. I gather my small backpack and step outside the car. I almost cry from the sheer enormity of the task. Both physical and emotional. Looking back at her, I can't help the question in my mind… *Why?*

And as if she can predict my thoughts, she throws out, "I have to go pick your brother up. I need to go now." She's saying she doesn't have the time to stay. But that's not true, is it? My brother is at school for the rest of the day. That's several more hours. And we both know it.

As if to justify this catastrophe of a morning, she gives me an anemic smile. I'll give it to her. She's trying. But nevertheless, it sets a deep pressure on my chest, full of hurt emotions.

I hear a cough followed by an "I'll see you soon." A "feel better" is slipped in there too. But it actually sounds more like she's saying, 'I'm done,' just arranged in more interesting letters.

I wait to hear something else, though it feels like I'm trying to put out the errant fires of our relationship with wishful thinking.

"I love you," I respond. It feels a bit synthetic, leaving a bad taste on my tongue.

The thing about starving myself – the thing about this debilitating fear of food and hatred toward my body that has led me to this very moment now – is that I've chipped away parts of me alongside my weight. And in this exact moment, I feel like I've chipped away something even bigger than that. *Is this actually all my fault? Maybe there is something horribly wrong with me…*

What happens next is a blur. I somehow make it to triage. Luckily, my doctor seemed to have called ahead to the ER. They knew I was coming. I am ever so grateful to be whisked away to an ER bed immediately, though I can't help but feel self-conscious after cutting an entire waiting room full of sick children. I lay there as they start IVs, set me up to the heart monitor and pulse ox, and the continuous blood pressure cuff. I let them know about this ache in my heart, but I don't have anything left in me to care or be concerned. It is the least of my problems. In reality, my mother hasn't been the most delicate with my heart. I shut out the anxiety around me and all the things they are trying to tell me that are wrong. I just garner enough strength to agree to be admitted to their medical unit.

Hours later, I'm lying in a big sterile room. It is colorfully decorated, as it is designed for children, though they seem to be okay with admitting up to 21 years too. The only company to my thoughts is the whirring of the IV pump, the daunting clattering of the feeding pump, and the uncomfortable gaze of the patient sitter in my room. I've deduced they think I can't be trusted alone. When my nurse comes in later to check up on things, and to quiet the incessant beeping of the heart rate monitor attached to the wall next to my bed, she asks how I feel. More specifically how my heart feels. I tremble a little bit when she slips in the words my mind had been so determinedly trying to block out.

Heart attack

Once she leaves, I go to grab my phone. And it does not escape me the amount of effort it takes to keep the thing in my hands. I didn't realize I was this weak.

I automatically go to press on the name that I've done so many times before. As I've done throughout my entire life. But as my thumb hovers over her contact, I can't help but get choked up. A cacophony of uncomfortable and contradicting emotions burns through me.

As I turn off my phone, burrow further beneath the thin and scratchy hospital blanket, and close my eyes, I realize that this is the end. I'm on my own with this. That I can't rely on anyone but myself. I realize that life has a way of abusing girls at their lowest possible moments, and so does my mother apparently. Comparison, and incidentally nostalgia for a better time in my life, is a thief of joy, though I can't help but yearn for a mom that cares selflessly for me. Yearning is as far as I'll ever get it seems.

I… God, I can't fucking breathe.

I can hear the thin veneer of our relationship shattering, and I can't help but hate myself for realizing this is how it's always been, and this is how it will always be. I held on to hope for nothing.

Contributors

Yuthaphong Angsuworaphuek, a final year Graphic Design student at Montgomery College, is a multilingual artist with a passion for 3D modeling, painting, drawing, and improving his human figure skills. Yuthaphong aims to become a 3D printing editor and cartoon character designer to showcase his creativity, and his dedication has already earned him recognition among his peers and teachers. With his unwavering commitment to excellence and artistic talent, Yuthaphong is poised to make a name for himself in the world of design.

Allan Bernal lives with his partner and pets, obsessing over movies and card games and ethical questions. He enjoys exploring themes of horror in his writing, but he doesn't like scary stuff really.

Alexander Beaudreau is a 20-year-old DC native who has been drawing and making clay and stone pieces for fun since he was a little kid. He took Drawing 1 at Montgomery College in Spring 2022, where he produced his Self Portrait among other pencil, ink, and charcoal pieces.

Alexandra Bouvier is a current student at Montgomery College, working toward earning an English degree at the University of Maryland. She has a passion for reading and works part-time as a preschool teacher's aide in Bethesda, MD.

Carina Cain is an artist who obtained her Associates in Fine Arts from Montgomery College. She is now at the University of Maryland continuing her education in the arts

ChatGPT needs no introduction.

Swift Dickison is professor of English at the Rockville Campus of Montgomery College, having taught there since 2001. Dr. Dickison is happy to remind AI and ChatGBT that, "whilst this machine is to him," he will relish any foil provided by a poetaster whose folly derives from its insistence upon "gathering the limbs of Osiris," with no sensibility regarding "the dancer" or "the dance."

Train Heist
Terry Quill

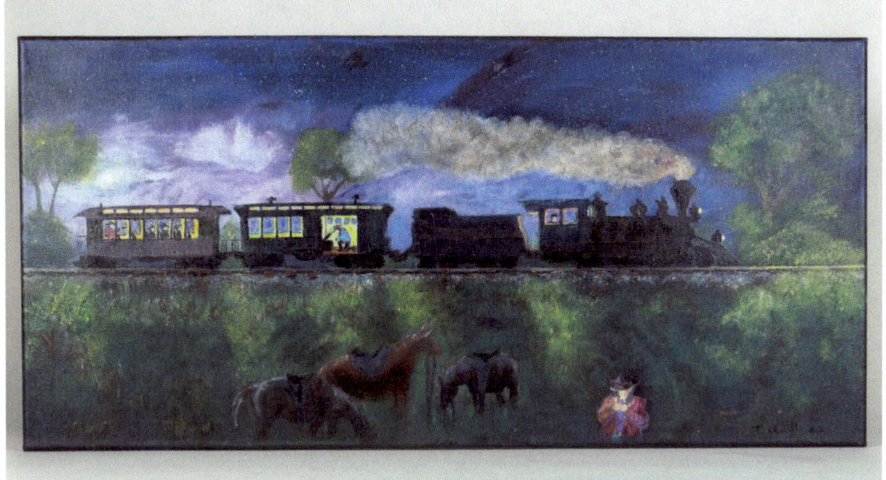

Blizzard
Samuel E. Obi

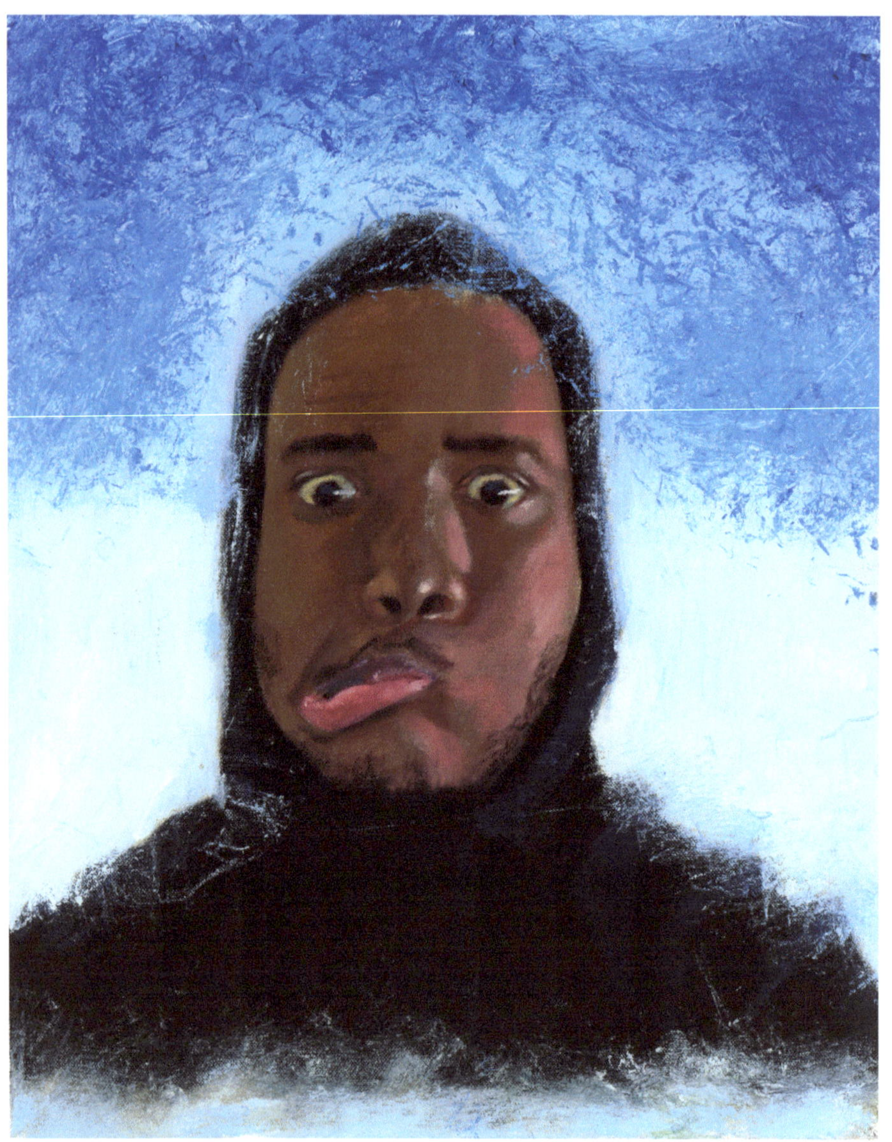

Niamh Ducey is an art student at Montgomery College, using art to show gratitude to people, communities and the environment. This "Giving Story" piece is a reminder that the act of giving can create life, inspire an idea, and motivate an action.

david alberto fernández is a poet from Miami, Florida who has lived for over 20 years "South of Sligo Creek" in Takoma Park, Maryland. He is the author of the poetry collections *Flowers beyond here* (2020) and *World consumes itself* (2021).

Marilyn Glass has a B.S. in Aerospace Engineering and MS in Technology Management. Once retired from engineering she began pursuing her passion for art as a student at Montgomery College. She is in the process of developing different techniques to distort images or use anamorphic art in new ways. She is primarily interested in painting and sculpting.

Li Howard is an art student at Montgomery College.

Nicolette Israel is an art student at Montgomery College.

Avery Johnston is an art student at Montgomery College.

Shelley Jones has taught Spanish at Montgomery College for 17 years and is one of the co-coordinators of the Global Classrooms Faculty Fellowship. She has long been a lover of poetry and she appreciates the unique opportunities of expression that poetry offers.

Maureen Feely Kohl's images come from a place of history, taking the opportunity to capture those things that are disappearing. These are mostly objects that have been discarded. Some stored away and then are forgotten. Her goal is to tell the stories of these artifacts by preserving them in a different way and medium.

Suzanne Maggi has studied printmaking at Montgomery College for the past seven years. She is a member of a printmaking collaborative studio in Takoma Park and of Ch/Art, a DC/MD community organization.

Ilana Maiman is a second year student at Montgomery College. When she isn't writing short stories, she can be found teaching Jewish religious school or rewatching the same TV show twelve times.

Luz Stella Mejía is a marine biologist, writer, and editor. She has published two books of poetry: *Etimologicas* and *Palabras Sumergidas*, and some of her short stories have been published in anthologies and magazines.

Barbara Milton is an art student at Montgomery College.

Fritz Mirand's painting is an excerpt of the history of his country, Haiti. He is very interested in selecting excerpts of the history of his country. This painting is an artistic presentation of the shipment of the great assistance that the Haitian president, Alexandre Sabes Petion, gave to Simon Bolivar to liberate the countries of South America from Spanish rule and slavery in 1815.

Neha Misra is a first-generation Indian American poet, a contemporary eco-folk visual artist, and an award-winning climate justice advocate. As an immigrant, Montgomery County in Maryland is her beloved adopted home. Neha is a Public Voices Fellow on the Climate Crisis with the OpEd Project in partnership with the Yale Program on Climate Change Communication to change who writes history.

Samuel E. Obi is an international student currently in Towson university. He is studying illustration with the goal of becoming a concept artist and designer. He mostly works on digital software, but in making this painting it somehow felt freeing. He hopes the passion put into the painting is well received.

Xin Ray Penland Obrien is working towards an Associates in Fine Arts. Growing up he lived in many different countries and was intrigued by Indonesian puppets (Wayang), Italian sculptures, and the scale of Chinese architecture.

Mary Ott is an art student at Montgomery College.

Terry Quill is a retired toxicologist and D.C. attorney who has always had an interest in the arts. Having a little time now to spend on new pursuits, he is enjoying visual arts with the help of Montgomery College. Terry takes advantage of a number of the College's introductory art classes, including printing, drawing and painting.

Giselle Ramos is an art student at Montgomery College.

Reed Reilly is a business major who loves writing. He is filled with ideas that he aspires to articulate fully through his fiction and non-fiction works. He loves to learn and get better at things, especially expressing these ideas. He has been writing for as long as he can remember and does it whenever the opportunity strikes.

Archie Brayer
Maureen Feely Kohl

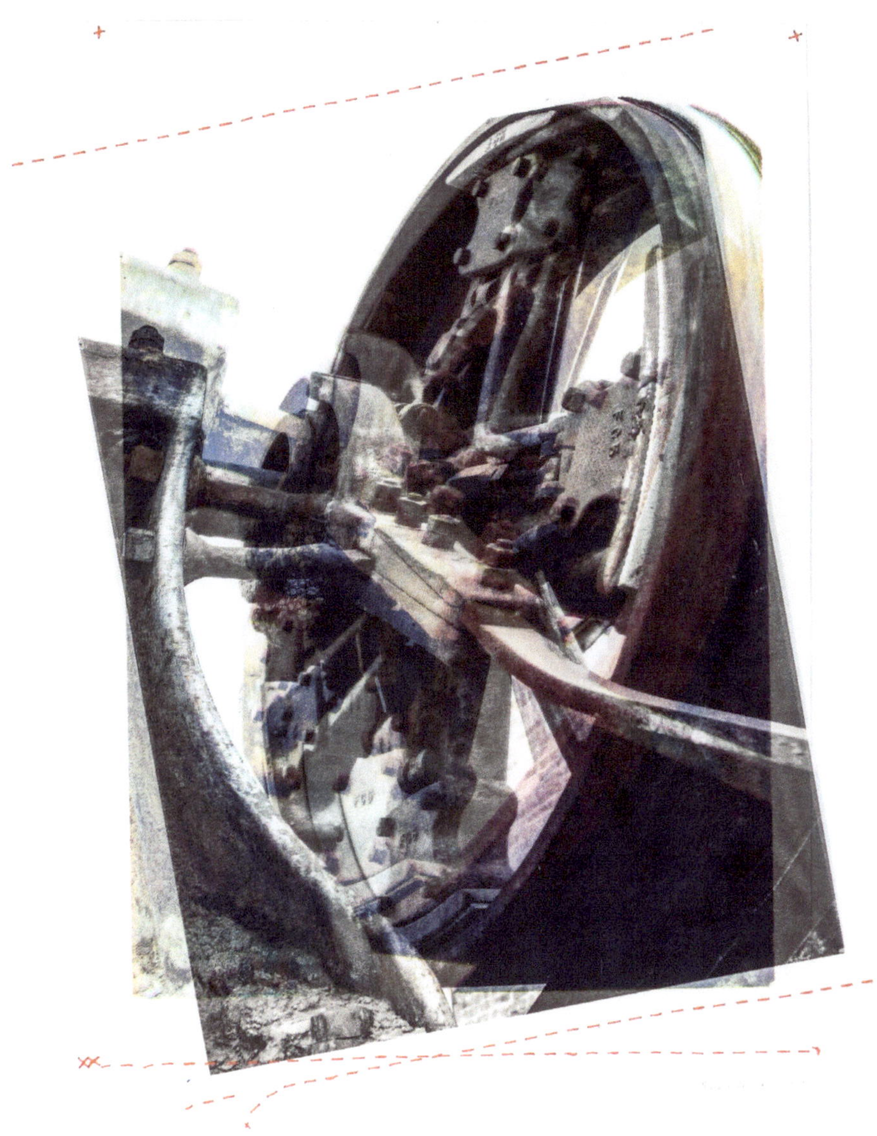

Heather Bruce Satrom has taught non-native speakers of English in the English Language for Academic Purposes program at Montgomery College since 2005. She recently returned to writing poetry and creative nonfiction after a long hiatus focused on parenting and teaching. She is currently working on an oral history project, documenting the lives of immigrant and refugee students at MC. She's also preparing to walk part of the Camino de Santiago and hopes to write lots of poems along the way.

Anaïs Llufire Siclla was born in Lima, Peru but lived longest in the Bronx, NY. Anaïs utilizes art as a means of self-expression.

Liat Suvorov is a fifty-one-year-old General Humanities student at Montgomery College, and wife and mother. Her poetry is inspired by her life experiences. Her poems "Be Like Water" and "Solid Ground" were published in *You Have Been Planted Here to Create Something Beautiful: An Anthology by Writers and Artists with Disabilities.*

Ted is a student poet who has asked to remain anonymous.

Miriam Zemen, originally from Puerto Rico, graduated from Yale University with a B.A. in Comparative Literature and obtained her M.A. in TESOL at American University. She currently coordinates the ESL Takoma Park/Silver Spring site and teaches courses in ESL, ELAP, and Spanish at MC.